IN THE BUNKERS
OF SINAI

IN THE BUNKERS OF SINAI

by *Arnold Sherman*

SABRA BOOKS · NEW YORK

Book designed by *Shimon Zendhaus*
Photographs by *Benny Hadar*

*This book could not have been written without the valuable
cooperation and support of a number of agencies and people.
Special thanks are due to the Army Spokesman and his office and
the men and officers of the Southern Command and to the Chief
Education Officer of Sinai and his staff. There are a number of
people who figured very prominently in this book from the ear-
liest stages: "Mannie" Steinberg who counselled; Yaffa Yarkoni
who contributed her time; Ami Perry who was a tireless support-
er of the project; Amiram Avrotsky who provided invaluable
data about the peninsula; Lev Bigon who supported the project
on the sturdy wings of Arkia aircraft; Harold Blumberg who
for some time now has been sublimating his own appreciable
writing talents on the thankless altar of galvanizing and shaping
the raw copy which this author has been churning out.*

ISBN 0–87631–042–0
LIBRARY OF CONGRESS CATALOG CARD NUMBER 73–133972
PRINTED IN ISRAEL
COPYRIGHT © 1971 AMERICAN ISRAEL PUBLISHING CO., LTD.

Contents

To Lucy,
who knows the apprehension of
every Israeli mother

Prologue

There is female softness in your bed. Her face is nearly concealed by the darkness, but enough moonlight intrudes into your bedroom to provide the woman with warm, familiar outlines and to tease shadows out of lifeless forms such as frozen lamps, a bouquet of flowers, an attaché case brimming with yesterday's problems, a letter from the principal complaining about your son's conduct, a book closed on a yellow pen.

You have been trying to sleep for hours, but it is impossible. You will never sleep this night.

The luminous face of your watch blinks a quiet message. It is 3 A.M. You have another hour before the alarm will crack the silence, commanding you to dress, check your knapsack, hook your canteen, strap on your combat boots—vintage 1952 Korean War—examine the Parabellum which already glistens with fresh oil, caress the sleeping shapes of the children who have already been alerted to the fact that you will not be there when they awaken hours later in order to bolt for school with marmalade and cocoa smeared across their faces, pat the head of the dog who will respond by waving his fluffy tail in an arc just once, and emerge through the night of tranquillity into the daylight of war. And you know that in dark households all over the country other men also begin this routine of separation from the ones they love.

This evening the Mediterranean provides its own special soliloquy. It is speaking about the two thousand year dream of a battered but resilient remnant. It is broadcasting the three wars, one in 1948 to etch the sand finger of Israel

13

into ecological reality, one in 1956 to prevent maritime strangulation and confirm the presence and viability of the besieged State, one in 1967 to prove the efficacy of the first Jewish State since Herod tumbled the ramparts of Jerusalem and the Star of David slid into its long ghetto twilight.

Since June 11, 1967, since the cease-fire which was no cease-fire, the Middle East has been a cauldron of bubbling, steaming military activity. Over three thousand Israelis, civilians and troops, men, women and children were slain or injured. Three thousand in a population of less than three million. More than one out of every thousand Israelis was killed or wounded in the most violent peace the world had known for some time. In the north, there were children who slept in bunkers adorned with Teddy bears and mortar shards. In the central regions, the blast of the Katyusha was a normal nocturnal punctuation. In the south, two strong and capable armies faced each other with steel teeth bared and mauled and maimed with splendid scientific regularity. And who knew what the death toll had been among the Arabs since the war was declared dead in 1967? Surely not less than 10,000 had perished.

In forty-five minutes you are at the airport. The terminal is filled with military uniforms, Uzzi submachine guns, revolvers; women bidding farewell to sons, fathers, husbands, lovers; military clerks checking arms, tired men blinking with fatigue, a pilot drinking coffee; layers of cigarette smoke, neon reflections.

The sun slides over the horizon as the loudspeaker announces the departure of your flight. Soon you are skybound, heading toward the center of a great desert, the first leg of a six-hour journey to the bunkers of the Sinai.

Down to the Line

When the night is moonless and both sides of the narrow ribbon of water are wrapped in a nearly impenetrable darkness, then tiny ends of starlight are caught in the almost motionless water and reflect off the ink surface like small bubbles of fire. There is a prevailing silence, not the silence of restful sleep but the silence of a jungle where great carnivorous cats, crouched over a water hole, are filtering even the faintest breaks in the silence through alert senses.

You hear the muffled cough of a vehicle being coaxed to life somewhere along the west bank of the Canal by nervous Egyptian hands, perspiring freely in the chilled desert air. On the east bank the intruding sound is reported by a helmeted shadow whispering into a walkie-talkie. He is told to keep a sharp eye on the area and report any additional sounds of activity immediately.

Now a dog barks across the isthmus and is soon joined by a canine chorus. To the trained ear, the meaning is clear: there is movement afoot. These wild dogs of Egypt are the unpaid sentinels of the Israeli army; you take note, and for a moment wonder how your dog at home is. As the animals growl, the cold, tired men behind sandbags and embankments stare westward across the darkness and finger the triggers of their weapons. Anchored to their positions a scant 250 meters away, Egyptian troops tighten their grips on their Kalachnikovs and wait for a response from the other side. Their ears too are alert, and their eyes are not less heavy with sleep.

Sleep—or the constant need of it—this is the brotherhood and agony of all soldiers, you think, your eyes beginning to close. But you are a writer, not a soldier, and you examine this tiredness which now overwhelms you as you would observe a stranger. Less than twenty-four hours ago, you were at home near Tel Aviv, joshing your wife over the sad state of the plumbing as she prepared hot coffee for your departure. You made the rounds of the bedrooms and kissed your three sleeping children goodbye. Staring into the darkness of the Sinai desert, you find it hard to believe that this is still the same long day. Is it possible to find such safety and comfort less than 200 miles away? Why had you assigned yourself to the bunkers of Sinai?

You recall your first stop on the way to Suez, just a week earlier: an orderly and spotlessly clean room in Tel Aviv. A large wall map tells the story of war and politics and patriotism and chauvinism in a splatter of timid colors.

"Our army can produce almost anything," says the officer, "but a quick cup of coffee."

"Aviva," he calls out, "are you making the coffee or picking the beans?"

Unruffled, private first class Aviva answers from the next room. "The water boils slowly even for a full colonel. Maybe it will boil quickly when you are a general."

"*Chutzpanit*," he says, smiling. "These Sabra females must always have the last word. God help my son when he grows up in another few years."

The phone rings and while the Colonel notes names and particulars on a pad, you scrutinize him. He is of medium height and lithe in build. He has gray hair and friendly eyes. His face is gentle despite the thin scar on the left side of his chin. You are meeting him to obtain basic information about the overall military situation at the Canal. This is your last stop before the front lines. There will be no more unhurried conversations, no more Avivas bringing coffee, no more academic discussions about the crisis in Sinai. Soon there will be the terror of exploding shells and the discomforts of the moving sands.

"You want to know about the Bar-Lev Line," says the Colonel, who began his military service in 1947 as a member of the Haganah and learned about Zionism and patriotism from his Bulgarian-born parents on a *kibbutz*. "Well, the first thing you should know is that the name is not ours. The term was supplied by our friends in Cairo. We never use that name in any of our official communications. It is true that the line was constructed during the tenure of our present Chief-of-Staff, General Chaim Bar-Lev, but we haven't given it any nicknames. So far as we are concerned, it is simply the Israel defense line along the Suez Canal."

He rises from his chair. "If you want to understand the military implications of the line, take a look at this map." He places his index finger on the narrow black ribbon between Africa and Asia.

"For both geographic and strategic reasons, the most vulnerable area in Sinai is the narrow border along the Suez Canal. This line is about 100 miles from north to south and parallels the Canal. This is the area where any major Egyptian breakthrough can take place and where the overwhelming bulk of the Egyptian forces is concentrated.

"I don't want to go too far back in history. You probably know all there is to know about the Six Day War. We were forced onto the battlefield in June 1967 and we won. When the cease-fire was finally declared, the troops of our Southern Command had captured all of the Sinai Peninsula with the single exception of a narrow strip of land near Port Fuad in the extreme north.

"From June 1967 until the autumn of 1968, the Suez line was comparatively quiet. There was a small amount of shelling, some sporadic sniping, but fundamentally the border with Egypt was a relatively manageable one.

"Egypt has never reconciled itself to any kind of peace with us, and with the incredible supply of new arms to Cairo from the Soviet Union, it was only a matter of time before the fighting would be triggered off again. That occurred in November 1968. Maintaining a vast superiority both in arms and in manpower, Egypt began a series of vicious artillery and mortar bombardments. Our troops were using only improvised dugouts on the border. The meaning was clear. We would have to dig deeply underground in order to survive and minimize our casualties. We're a small nation and we couldn't afford the luxury of seeing dozens of our men blown to pieces in unprotected areas. It was obvious to us even then that we were at war.

"A decision to create a fixed defense line is not a simple one. It represents all sorts of tactical, strategic and financial considerations. It was never our intention to build another Maginot Line. We knew that our financial and manpower resources prevent us from hermetically sealing off the Canal. The initial decision was made at General Headquarters and received the blessings and support of the Government. We had to consult with dozens of different military agencies. Such questions as where to erect the forts, their geographical deployment, the types of defense weapons to be used, locations of gun emplacements and observation platforms had to be answered."

There is another phone call. The Colonel jots something down and passes it to Aviva.

"Understand," he goes on, "that Zahal [the Israel Defense Forces] was new to the game of static defense. It was a concept diametrically opposed to all our ideas and training. Because of our limited manpower and resources, we had always emphasized extreme mobility, and it was this tactic that helped win our wars with the Arabs. Strike hard and fast was our credo."

You recall an explanation that you had heard from another military officer just before the Six Day War. "The Arabs are neither cowards nor fools," he had said, "but they are mercurial. They heat up quickly and they cool off fast. The only way for Israel to destroy an Arab army is by sheer impetus. The same concept was employed by the Romans and used by the Germans during World War II for the blitz. Once Zahal commits itself to a plan of action, it must move forward relentlessly. That is why we are such firm advocates of armor. If ever we are fought to a stalemate, the Arabs will draw our blood."

The Colonel continues, "The concept of the defense line was an awesome one. Just the investment alone staggers the imagination, particularly within the economic framework of a poor country like Israel. But we really didn't have any alternative. The Suez Canal was a natural boundary between both sides and it wouldn't have been feasible for us to strike out in force at the west side. Even if we could have withstood the political pressures, the losses would have been appalling.

"The Egyptian line was prepared with Soviet connivance and assistance. The ratio of Egyptian to Israeli guns is twenty-five to one. In terms of committed manpower on the Canal alone, it is thirteen to one."

The Colonel makes no further comment but you remember Western reports indicating that about 10,000 Israeli troops defend the line. This would place the Egyptian forces on the west bank at 130,000 men. With at least another 150,000 troops directly behind the frontline Egyptian forces, it would be no exaggeration to place the estimate of overall Egyptian forces facing Israel at well over a quarter of a million.

"The Egyptians knew we were up to something once we started construction, but they never realized the enormity of our undertaking. Most of the tractor work was conducted under heavy Egyptian fire. Only when we had managed to complete sand ramparts which blocked Egyptian observation and provided a measure of protection against snipers and shells were we in a slightly less vulnerable position and able to begin more sophisticated construction activity.

"As a matter of fact, the construction continues to this very day. We are continually building, repairing and modernizing. So long as we are committed to holding the Canal, we will do everything humanly possible to minimize casualties. We are heartbroken about the losses that have occurred, but I hate to think about what would be going on now if our boys were in more vulnerable and exposed positions."

"Excuse me," interrupts Aviva. "Shmuel wants to know when you will have a few moments for him."

"Tell Shmuel soon. And where is the coffee?"

"You've already had two cups. Want to poison yourself?"

"A good description of her coffee," he confides amiably and resumes; "in addition to the actual construction, we had to learn a whole new system of tactics. We had to explain to commanders who had been weaned on the philosophy of mobility that they had to remain fixed, that the initiative was oftentimes with the enemy. The explanation was made simpler for us by the political facts of life. The policy of the Government of Israel is not to give up an inch until we achieve a political settlement.

"The defense line was constructed according to the capabilities of the Jews of Israel. We knew then and we know now that we cannot match the Arabs in numbers of soldiers, fire power or armor. The line was created to provide military answers to two basic needs: first, to prevent the possibility of a major Egyptian assault on Sinai with the consequent creation of a bridgehead which could lead to an all-out war; and, second, to reduce as much as possible the casualties among the defending troops.

"This does not mean," he adds hastily, "that small Egyptian units cannot penetrate among our positions. They have done so in the past and they undoubtedly will continue to do so. Now and then small enemy forces manage to cross over in order to lay ambushes, attack our communications, place mines. This is regrettable but we have never claimed that the defense line made Sinai impervious to isolated Egyptian ground attacks. What is important is that Egyptian forces have never succeeded in storming a fortress. On occasion, they reached the outer perimeters of the forts, but they have never penetrated inside the enclosures."

You tell him you saw the photograph released by Cairo some time ago showing victorious Egyptian soldiers standing under the Egyptian flag on the east bank of the Canal in one of the Israeli forts. You checked and were informed that the fort was indeed an Israeli citadel, but a deserted one.

"The Egyptian situation is quite different," the Colonel points out. "North of Kantara, for example, Egyptian emplacements cover every inch of the Canal, both in terms of visual observation and fire power. We have no illusions about being able to compete with them on this score.

"Our line is much more flexible than you might think. It is really much more than a static line of strategically located outposts. It is an entire defense system which contains a built-in offensive capability. The forts are located at strategic points but they are supported by highly mobile armor contingents that patrol the gaps in our positions and are ready for immediate deployment in the event of attack. In addition, we have the third component of highly mobile artillery units—and our strike force, of course, the Air Force. These four elements comprise our military capability along the Canal.

"Our decision to use our air power against Nasser

was a response to increasing Egyptian activity along the Canal, which escalated sharply in March of '69. During the first year of the Suez conflict, between June '67 and June '68, there had been 104 incidents.

"During the next year the incidents soared to 1,007. That was the end of June '69.

"The next month we introduced our air element as the most successful method of answering the Egyptian challenge. We had two fundamental objectives in mind. We had to enable our ground forces to hold the line, and to de-escalate the danger of out-and-out war, by attacking the Egyptian military infra-structure. First and foremost we had to secure freedom of operation for our aircraft by destroying every ground-to-air missile site in the Canal area. And by the 'Canal area' I mean every emplacement within twenty miles of the cease-fire line. This was no easy objective, incidentally, because the sites were well protected by over 1,500 antiaircraft guns which provided low-level defense against air attack. Simultaneously, the Air Force was attacking other assorted ground targets, mainly gun emplacements.

"Within three to four months from the time we began air operations, the first objective was completely achieved. Not a single SAM site remained operational in the Canal zone.

"And while this was going on, our planes were attacking Egyptian gun positions as well. As a direct consequence of the commitment of air power, Israeli losses went down.

"By the fall of '69," continues the Colonel, "life had become a good deal easier for our troops in Sinai, although there was never really any lull in the fighting.

"In January '70 we began our next phase of operations, to achieve our second óbjective. We went out to hit military targets deeper in Egypt. We initiated this second stage of air activity to actually prevent a new war. Our motto had been 'live and let live,' but since this message was lost on Nasser we had no alternative but to attack the Egyptian war machine where it would really hurt.

"We know that the deep-penetration raids succeeded and effectively frustrated the Egyptian preparations for an all-out attack against us. We destroyed army stores near Cairo, military base camps where troops were being deployed, and vital communications. As a direct result, the Egyptians had to move their military academy to the Sudan and their naval school to Libya. Egyptian military concentrations were dispersed. A possible war was prevented—or at least postponed. This is not idle conjecture on our part. Egyptian War Minister Fawzi freely admitted at that time that Egypt was organizing its forces for an all-out war."

He pauses for a moment, his face suddenly solemn. "Now the situation has changed again. With Soviet pilots and rocket technicians actively protecting the interior of Egypt, we have been forced to curtail our activities. As a result of this development and the huge amounts of Russian aid being poured into Egypt, Cairo is once again free to mobilize for war. That they are doing so is something they don't even bother to deny.

"There is nothing new about the Russian involvement in the Middle East," he says. "They have been here for a long time. I would be a fool, however, if I said that we are happy about recent developments. They have admitted that their pilots are flying missions for the Egyptian Air Force. Soviet naval strength in the area is no secret. More and more Soviet military advisers have been arriving. They have undertaken and have completed a number of significant and strategic construction activities such as the SAM-3 missile sites.

"What I can say is that our morale is as high as ever. Our troops know their missions and they will execute them fully. We will maintain our positions along the Canal, no matter what happens and no matter who attacks. This holds true for our ground forces and for our Air Force. If Russia takes a more active part in the conflict, everyone of us knows his duty. We say it clearly and openly—we will fight. This will not be another Czechoslovakia. Perhaps if we take an unequivocal stand, the Russians will understand the issues at stake. Of course, while we all know our duty, the real answer lies in Washington. When it comes to deterring the Russians and preventing a real holocaust in this area, America is the key factor.

"However, as far as Egypt is concerned—and Egypt is our main enemy—we are confident that, despite their rearming, we can foil any of their attempts to form a bridgehead in Sinai."

And what of the future, you ask. He nods his head, expecting the question.

"It will be a long siege. It will take a very long time. We are bleeding but, considering the type of battle we are fighting, the losses are comparatively small. What hurts us is that our country is small and the loss of every life is a personal blow.

"The defense line is not the last and only answer.

Although we have prevented an Egyptian attack, we are still suffering casualties. Our boys are still being killed. But whatever our losses, we will hold firm along the Canal. We will not retreat one inch.

"Why am I confident? I will tell you. It is because I believe in the Jewish people, not only the Jews of Israel but the Jews of the entire world. I have an almost mystical faith in them and I am confident that as long as they remain steadfast, we will remain strong."

"Hey! Have an orange." You open your eyes and a young trooper with faint fuzz on his face thrusts the fruit into your hand. "I thought you were sleeping standing up," he says.

"No, I closed my eyes for just a second," you answer uncertainly. "I was thinking about some other place."

"I know," he says. "I often find myself thinking about home. Today I kept thinking about my sister. I don't know why. I never really liked her."

You peel the orange. You suddenly feel very cold and tired.

"Nothing like an orange to clean the sand out of your mouth," says your new friend.

You agree. "How old are you?" you ask.

"I'll be 19 tomorrow."

You pull out some mentholated candy your daughter gave you.

"Happy birthday," you wish him and offer him some.

Popcorn and Shells

The fortress overlooking the rusting El Firdhan Bridge is a dark shape in the moonlight. You stare intently into the deep shadows, and certain carefully etched contours begin to emerge. As you approach, you detect the great wall of sandbags and trenches that run along the perimeter. You already know where the entrances to the cavernous bunkers are located, where the accordion rolls of barbed wire are situated. You detect a single, tiny light, filtering out through black curtains where the mess hall is moored to a floor of sand.

The man inside the mess hall thinks he is alone but he is deceived. Safe in the shadows are four large hungry rats, their noses puckered at the smell of cooking food.

Once, during the lean days before the Six Day War, these rats dominated the evening landscape on the east side of the Canal, but those were the hard times before Israeli troops stepped into the area. Now, with leftovers and scraps strewn about, the rodents of Sinai are enjoying a prosperity which their kind has not seen for perhaps thousands of years. Over the past three years, they have built up a justifiable confidence, sleeping during the day and safe from pursuit and destruction at night when sounds of a struggle would jeopardize troop positions.

The man is busily popping corn. In the curtained light he could pass for any soldier anywhere along the length of the Israeli positions on the Canal. He wears the same sand-flecked boots, the same work clothes, the same drab wool sweater to keep the cold from his lean frame. But even in the flickering light of the kitchen, there is an apparent difference: his receding hair is silver and his thin face is creased. At fifty-two, the doctor is perhaps the oldest soldier on the line. You are pleased that he is there. You feel not quite so old yourself.

This South African M.D. protests very vigorously if accused of being a Zionist.

"I knew that South Africa was not the place where I wanted to bring up my family," he says. "There seemed to be two possibilities—to immigrate to England or to Israel. To be quite honest, after we left Johannesburg I gave England a chance for two years. We might have remained there were it not for one thing—our three children. Having tried life in Israel, they were miserable in England. They felt passionately identified with this country. There didn't seem to be any choice.

"To tell you the truth I didn't fight their decision very hard. I too feel more at home here. It seems to provide me with a purpose, more direction to my life. I have never regretted the decision, nor have my children. My oldest boy is a pilot in the Air Force and so is my son-in-law. And my younger son—he's sixteen now—has joined a kibbutz up north. He's very serious about it. He hopes to become a full-fledged member when he finishes his studies."

While he talks the doctor shovels the popcorn into a large crate which had held oranges.

"This whole business of popcorn is really quite interesting," he remarks. "About a month ago, one of the boys received a present of a bag of dried corn kernels. He tasted a few and found them indigestible. He mentioned it to me, and I explained that the raw corn had to be popped first and showed him how to do it. It was a great success—with all the boys, too. You have no idea how it's boosted our morale.

"I asked my wife to send me about ten bags immediately. She thought I was crazy and begged me to see a doctor. Now we're up to our ears in popcorn. It's a regular treat. If the boys didn't get their share every night, they'd be disappointed."

The doctor finishes ladling the popcorn into the crate and carefully turns off the flame. Two large rats pounce on a few stray kernels, greedily devour them and rush back into the shadows.

The doctor carefully folds an elastic stretch belt and places it on top of the crate. Then, one arm hugging the box and the other cradling an Uzzi, he steps out into the Sinai evening.

"Nu Moshe," he says, crawling into the first observation post, "how goes it?"

"Fine, Doctor," answers the chilled soldier.

"How's the splinter in your finger?"

"I think it's infected."

"Come to see me first thing tomorrow morning. OK, Moshe, you know what you have to do now."

"Oh, no," protests Moshe. "My muscles are still sore from last night."

"Moshe," says the doctor sternly, "do you want the popcorn or not? Because if not, there are at least a dozen men who would be more than glad to relieve you of the problem."

Moshe sighs resignedly and gently places his weapon against a sandbag. He reaches into the box and takes out the elastic belt and then quickly grabs a few kernels of corn and pops them into his mouth.

The doctor gently raps Moshe's hand. "You're going to turn into a gangster, you know, if you keep this up. A deal is a deal. Now—twenty times."

"Ten," protests Moshe. "I ache all over. You're killing me."

"Twenty," retorts the doctor, "or I'll have you barred from the PX as well."

Moshe stretches the elastic belt across his chest. "Fifteen?" he asks meekly, having reached eight stretches.

"Twenty," insists the doctor.

Moshe completes his ordeal and is rewarded with two handfuls of hot salted popcorn.

"You're worse than the Egyptians," he laughs. "They only want to kill me. You want to ruin me. Anyway, thanks for the popcorn. Goodnight, Doctor."

The doctor stops outside the next post. The dogs on the other side of the Canal are barking, and a soldier with binoculars is staring into the darkness.

"Did you speak to your family, Shmulik?" the doctor asks him.

"Didn't have a chance to call."

"Has your sister given birth yet?"

"Any day now," answers the soldier, reaching automatically in the meantime for the elastic belt.

"Do you realize that you're going to be an uncle?"

"Yeah," answers Shmulik.

"That's quite a responsibility."

"What am I supposed to do?" asks Shmulik as he counts to eleven.

"You're supposed to behave like an uncle—that's what you're supposed to do."

"Doctor, I had a pain in my chest this afternoon. Can you have a heart attack when you're nineteen?"

"It's a well-known fact in this fortress that you have no heart."

"Stop kidding, Doctor."

"Gas," the doctor opines.

"Gas?"

"Gas!"

As the doctor approaches the next station, there is a low whoomp from the other side of the Canal. The soldier on duty announces an incoming shell. The doctor cradles the popcorn and wheels in the direction of the command bunker. There are only seconds to find cover before the shell lands. On an incline some of the popcorn spills to the ground.

"The rats will have a party tonight," grumbles the doctor as he reaches the entrance to the bunker. Seconds later an 82-mm. mortar explodes, and the ground near the latrine erupts in a geyser of sand.

"Those guys on the other side have something against popcorn," mutters the doctor. "They do it every time."

In the bunker the doctor removes his helmet and offers some of the food to the tired men. Head of a new department at Hadassah Hospital in Jerusalem, the doctor is performing his reserve duty. The lot of an Israeli doctor has never been an easy one. In addition to long hours and modest pay, he can look forward to at least one month a year with the troops.

"It doesn't bother me at all to be here," the doctor says. "As a matter of fact, I am seriously thinking of volunteering for a year's service. Zahal is terribly short of medical personnel, and I could arrange the year's leave from my post with Hadassah without much difficulty. I feel very much at home with these boys, and it's not just a matter of performing my medical duties. Somehow they welcome the presence of an older man in an outpost like this, so far removed from everything familiar to them. It's good for me too. I feel younger since I got here."

The red bulb of the radio flashes an incoming transmission. Farther south, movement has been sighted on the Canal. A small force of Egyptian commandos is planning to ford the narrow river with rubber boats. They must be intercepted. All the fortresses linked to command headquarters coordinate activities and plans. Every movement is carefully programmed and cleared to foil the Egyptians' chances for laying a mine or an ambush.

"What could I do?" he shrugs. The doctor is talking again. "We're shorthanded here, and the boys work very hard. When I arrived a month ago I discovered that we had an abundance of good food, the facilities for cooking, but no cook. So I became the chief chef of Firdhan. Of course, it's possible to turn a driver or mortar man into a cook, but the result is very indifferent cooking. You know, life in a fortress is not like life in the civilian world. Outside, there are many diversions and comforts—a movie or theater or a good restaurant. Food in a fortress takes on a new meaning. It's not only im-

36

portant to stuff yourself—it's important to enjoy what you're eating.

"Take the business of a simple fruit salad. We have plenty of fresh fruit here. Now you can either provide a man with a banana in the morning, an orange at midday and an apple at night or you can do something interesting. With the least bit of ingenuity and a little work, you can produce an excellent fruit salad. I know. I'm considered the best fruit salad-maker in the whole Canal area."

The radio vibrates again. The reported commando landing is being checked. Troops on observation points are instructed to double their vigilance.

"There's another point," the doctor continues. "If a doctor is lucky, then life here tends to be monotonous. What I mean is this—we worry about health, we worry about hygiene, and we have to take care of the wounded. Once you've created the proper standards for health and hygiene, then you find you have time on your hands—that is, if you're fortunate and don't have many wounded. It would be a pity to waste that time when everyone is on a twenty-four-hour alert. That's why I cook.

"I don't want to give you the impression that I'm another Chef Nicolai, but on the other hand I can piece together a fairly palatable meal."

"Enough of that mock modesty," interjects one of the officers, looking up from a desk made of salvaged wooden crates. "Not only is he our chief father confessor, popcorn maker and chef, but he participates in early morning patrols as well. Wait till you see him wearing his flak jacket and carrying his Uzzi. We want to keep him protected from enemy fire, so he has strict instructions to crouch low in his carrier, even if it is armored."

"Look here," explains the doctor. "I'm not only a medical man—I'm also a soldier. What sort of respect would the boys have for me if I hid inside a bunker all the time? Patrolling is part of life here."

There is a sudden sharp slap. Zvika, the eighteen-year-old radio operator, has smacked a mosquito on his forehead. He looks momentarily dazed from the blow.

"Damn these mosquitoes. Look at them tonight!" The doctor points to the huge swarm of insects around the single bulb burning in the bunker. "They built up an immunity to DDT generations ago and now they spurn every type of local spray. These are the type that transmit malaria—the anopheles—and without preventive pills the entire line would have gone down with the disease long ago. There's malaria on the other side of the Canal, and mosquitoes can't read border signs."

The radio starts up again. An unidentified vehicle sighted in the north is moving along the road without lights. There is a hurried check with all centers. Within a few moments it is identified as an armored personnel carrier evacuating a soldier with acute appendicitis. The radio clicks off.

The doctor asks the fortress commander if he had perhaps spoken to his wife earlier in the day. The officer, a tall, regular army officer whose family had been merchants in Libya before they emigrated to Israel, answers affirmatively.

"I try to get word back to her every day. She's a Yecke,* you know. She worries. So why should I give

* An Israeli of German birth. In the vernacular, the word means a person who is terribly proper and formal.

her more worries than necessary?"

He looks down at the papers on his desk and picks them up reluctantly. "They're turning me into a clerk," he says good-naturedly.

"I feel as though my eyes are pasted together," says the doctor. "Is there anything I can do Major, before I turn in? I want to get some sleep before the morning patrol."

The Major nods his head. "No, Doctor. Go get some rest. You look tired. You're making too many fruit salads."

The Public Garden

It is 7 A.M. and the Sinai sun is peeking through a bank of cumulous clouds and slowly burning away the early morning fog rising over the still waters of the Canal.

There has been an increase of enemy aircraft activity during the past few days. Only the day before two Sukhoi 7s, flying on the deck, had laid two 500-pound bombs squarely in the area of the citadel. Fortunately, no one had been hurt, and orders had been given to erect a new latrine around one of the craters.

"This was one of the rare occasions," says Major Aaron, the youthful commander of the base opposite Ismailia, "when the enemy actually succeeded in saving us some work."

Tall, ginger-haired and blue-eyed, the thirty-four-year-old Major had been a career officer in the paratroops and armored corps for many years before he left to enter a family contracting business in Rishon LeZion.

"Why did I leave the army, particularly when I admit that by nature I am a professional army man? I'll tell you. I have three children—two girls, nine and seven, and a son only a year and a half old. I loved the army and always felt a part of it, but army life is not compatible with family life. I've been married thirteen years, and I decided that it was time that I spent more of my life with my wife and children.

"I'm here today as a volunteer. You see, I was invited to a meeting at which the Defense Minister and the Chief-of-Staff spoke about the need for competent officers to command these units. I have certain specialized skills to contribute, and as an Israeli who loves his country I didn't really seem to have a choice. So I volunteered for two months.

"In many ways this is harder than anything I've experienced before. The logistics problems are enormous, and there's a lot of responsibility.

"Yes, I was wounded. My wife still doesn't know about it. A 60-mm. mortar shell caught me as I was diving into a bunker. I've been limping a bit but by the time I finish my present tour of duty, the wounds should be completely healed."

Danger and hardship are no new elements to Aaron who was a free-fall expert in the paratroops and a leader of a mobile commando unit in the Negev.

"My purpose here is to hold the line. I retaliate only when necessary. I don't want casualties. I'm not underestimating the potential or cunning of the enemy, but I believe that we're quite competent to foil any and all of their offensive efforts.

"What's my role here? I guess I do a little of everything. My natural place is at the observation posts whenever there's trouble—and there's almost always trouble. Then there is a tremendous number of other factors: morale, supplies, tactics, coordination, reports, manual labor. My most important consideration, however, is the knowledge that maps don't mean a damn thing. Wherever we are, wherever our flag flies, there is Israel. That's the only vital consideration.

"We must rid the Egyptians of their taste for war. We must punish their attacks. We must demonstrate that we will not be unseated from these citadels no matter what the losses and no matter how difficult the conditions. I live with the feeling that directly behind me is Rishon LeZion."

Your conversation with Aaron is interrupted by an urgent call from one of the sentry posts: "An incoming shell!" Everyone, including a soldier wearing phylacteries and midway through his morning prayers, dives towards the nearest bunker. The shell lands about eighty yards away. Orders are sent to return the fire, and soon the entire encampment is belching smoke.

Meanwhile inside the bunkers the soldiers amuse themselves by talking about how they will spend their next leave.

The bunkers are long, narrow tubes protected by tons of earth and reinforced steel and equipped with electricity and phones. They are safe, but they are anything but comfortable. There is little room for maneuvering between the double-decker bunks lining the sides. If two fully equipped soldiers meet midway, one has to flop on the nearest bunk to let the other pass.

Uzzis and other weapons dangle from every hook. Throughout the fortress there is an abundance of movie posters, drawings, paintings and postcards tacked up to every available spot. There is a surprising lack of "cheesecake," and a complete absence of salacious art work.

Even before the shower of missiles ends, the battalion commander arrives with his entourage of two jeeps on a surprise inspection of the citadel. He is lithe and intense. He is also angry. He has caught one of the soldiers without his steel helmet on in an exposed area.

"You idiot," he roars. "Stand at attention when I speak to you. It would serve you right to lose that stupid head of yours."

He turns to Aaron. "Is this an indication of how you run your unit?" he sputters. Without giving Aaron a chance to reply, he stares fixedly at the trooper and then sentences him to thirty-five days in the stockade.

The battalion commander then enters the command bunker and roars about the "disorderliness."

"What are these crates doing here?" he demands to know as he kicks an empty ammunitions case to the side. He calls all the noncommissioned officers to the bunker.

"Discipline here is disgraceful," he says as the men stand at attention. "The entire fortress is sloppy. None of you will be going on holiday until further notice.

"Sit down," he orders as he lights a cigarette. He proceeds to ask the men theoretical questions on what they would do should the Egyptians succeed in infiltrating the inner defenses of the base. Satisfied with the answers, he releases the men and smiles at Aaron.

"You have a good bunch of men," he confides. "Keep them safe."

Outside, the sun is climbing and the shadows are growing thinner across the Canal. There is the sweet smell of boiling coffee and the promise of a belated breakfast. You make your way to the tiny mess room and kitchen. A lamentable structure at best, it is called the Laughing Indian Night Club. As a suitable decor, the walls are covered with posters inviting travelers to visit

46

Portugal and San Francisco. There are many signs, written in English: "Saloon," "Whiskey," "Hotel." You also notice broad Latin letters painted across the width of the kitchen reading "Public Garden" and an arrow pointing in the direction of the Canal.

You peer from the kitchen in the direction the arrow points and you see the public garden is an area of less than a square yard. In keeping with the environment, it is a collection not of flowers and trees but of shells and multicolored fragments which have rained down on the fortress from the other side of the Canal. About a dozen specimens are planted in the dirty gray soil under the heading of "Egyptian Sinai Roses." Since any garden requires a degree of diversification, there are three nearly ruined potato plants on the outer edge of the garden near a faded wicker fence and a few onion plants already fainting from the morning heat. The garden is spotlessly clean.

It gives you great pleasure to discover in one of the world's harshest and most debilitating environments, this testament to man's ability to smile.

The High Cost of Construction

The conclusion of the Six Day War had triggered a unique set of challenges for the Engineers. In addition to the customary tasks of minefield clearance and military construction, a new defense line had to be erected along the entire length of the Canal. Egypt was strong in artillery and even wealthier in disposable manpower. By 1968, heavy Russian-built guns were hammering away at semi-exposed Israeli positions relentlessly. Zahal responded, but the war of attrition favored the army of the Nile: Every dead Israeli soldier cut into the fabric of Israel. A dozen dead Egyptians meant nothing but more propaganda for Cairo.

Valuable lives could have been saved by relying on occasional patrols to preserve the Israeli presence on the east bank, but this would have been a useless and self-defeating ploy since in the long run it would pave the way for even fiercer fighting and even greater numbers of Israeli casualties. Egyptian commando forays were already forcing an Israeli reply. Unless the Israeli flag flew on the water's edge, Egyptian forces would be free to penetrate deep into Sinai and to undermine the occupation. The Arabs would weave a net of mines and ambushes. Israeli communications and transportation would be hampered and even severed. If permitted, with their new amphibious equipment, the Egyptians would not only ford the narrow strip of water separating the opposing sides but consolidate their forces on the east bank and prepare for an all-out confrontation on Israeli-held territory.

There was no choice. Israel had to retain its foothold on its very perimeters. It would have to stake out its claim along the narrow cleft between the two continents of Africa and Asia. There would be manpower losses. There would be the maimed and the dead, but the alternative was even more grave and awesome. The Canal was a natural border. The Israeli presence would have to be preserved. For the first time in history, Zahal would have to erect and hold a static defense line. The offensive capability, the strategy of punishment, would have to be handed over to the Air Force.

The Bar-Lev Line is an incredible testimonial to the Israeli fighting man's endurance and dedication, but it is also one of the most awesome engineering feats in the country's history. With often only seventy yards separating the antagonists, tremendously outnumbered in terms of manpower, severely outgunned by the latest in Russian artillery batteries, facing not only the compact might of Egyptian infantry, artillery and armor but contingents of Sudanese, Algerians and Kuwaitis, the Isreali army dug in.

But how do you build and ferret into the protective sand when you are within conversing range of an overwhelmingly larger enemy? How do you carve fortresses out of an exposed landscape when every movement is obvious? How do you create a defensive wall, with an absolute minimum of casualties, under a lethal rain of shells and mortars? In short, how do you survive?

The mission was assigned to the Engineering Corps. The Israeli positions on the bank of the Canal would be preserved by a network of strategically located bastions which would not only protect the Israeli flanks but govern the vital arteries that define suzerainty over the peninsula—the Via Maris stretching from Kantara to El Arish and Gaza, the roadway originating at Ismailia in the center of the Canal, crossing over the El Firdhan Bridge and connecting with Bir Gafgafa and the Negev, and the Suez route leading out to Mitla and forking across toward Eilat.

Whoever controlled these three vital arteries governed Sinai and its 68,000 square kilometers of wasteland. Whoever controlled Sinai preserved a major tactical advantage both in the air in terms of advance air bases and on the ground in respect to armor deployment.

There was no question but that the fortresses would have to be built. The Israeli presence would have to be buttressed by a great coat of sand and steel stretching along the entire length of the Canal. True, Sinai would not be hermetically sealed from the enemy. True, small and inconsequential commando units might still get across but these forays would only be pinpricks and not of decisive importance.

To cut down on losses, the tractors, caterpillers and other earth-moving equipment operated in the starlight— even a full moon could be dangerous—and as the sun swung over the horizon in the morning, a perceptible change could be discerned in the harsh, blank landscape. Overnight, walls of protective sand began rising to blind the enemy and safeguard the defenders. And behind the curtain, the stage was set for sophisticated construction activities—the creation of the forts themselves. For this Herculean task, the Engineering Corps was mobilized to the last drop of its military adrenalin. Every available man and machine was earmarked for the Bar-Lev Line. And even that was not enough, and so civilian contractors were hired. One of these was Eli.

Eli felt nothing but the thin winter sunlight caressing the black, one-day stubble on his face. It almost amused him for a moment when the tractor continued in reverse, like a horseless rider, until it backed into a sand dune and miserably sputtered to a halt.

Several micro-seconds earlier, twenty-year-old Eli was remembering the voice of the army doctor at the recruiting station in Petah Tikva who was patiently explaining that Eli's lungs were better but not entirely healed and that it would take a little while longer until he would be accepted into Zahal. "A little while longer," seemed like too long a time. Patience is not one of the virtues of youth.

So Eli had volunteered. He had been temporarily denied his turn in the ranks. Working at the Canal was at least a small dispensation until the day he could wear a uniform. And that day would be the happiest day of his life.

"I hope you know what the hell you're doing, Eli," the officer had said to Eli, the civilian contractor, as he twirled the stub of a worn pencil. "It's not going to be a picnic. The casualties are already high and the situation is going to get worse. You will be working from exposed positions. I suggest you think some more about this. Have a talk with your folks. Don't do anything rash.

The pay is good, but a dead man is just as dead with a pocketful of money."

One of Eli's six brothers was already serving in the Engineering Corps and he would follow in his footsteps. The thought of not being with his boyhood friends, his *hevra*, his company from the *moshav*, was more than he could stand. Having been raised in a farm community and already an experienced tractor driver, Eli would have no trouble gaining admission to the Engineers. There was a great deal to be done on the Canal, seriously hampered by a shortage of experienced personnel.

Eli took a deep breath and it hurt right up to the roots of his hair. Something attracted his attention. His right arm was shredded. It seemed to be attached by only a thin, red ribbon of flesh. "So stupid," he thought through the shock. "So damn stupid."

Eli had finished his work the night before—most of the construction had to be done in the safety of evening and only occasional activities were undertaken in daylight. Although Eli was scheduled to return home on leave shortly, special work had kept him there. It was not Eli's turn on the tractor; he had volunteered to replace a friend.

"This shouldn't have happened," he thought. "It couldn't happen."

Slowly, Eli focused his eyes on the approaching shadow of the soldier who only moments before had been acting as his observer. Their eyes met for a second and he saw horror.

He wanted to say something, but his tongue was caught between his teeth. "My arm is gone," he forced himself to think, "but I am not going to die."

Not too far away, a jeep zigzagged through the sand, racing toward the womblike protection of one of the fortresses. The driver was a curly-haired, gum-chewing private with a band of freckles running down his face. Seated next to him was a twenty-eight-year old lieutenant, a veteran of the Six Day War. The lieutenant was pre-occupied with his thoughts. He was musing over his wife and year-old daughter. He was also thinking of his planned vacation to Europe. He had been born in Petah Tikva and had never ventured out of Israel. Reaching Europe had become an obsession for him. He and his wife had been assiduously saving their money. In another few months there would be enough and then he would realize one of the major ambitions of his life.

In the back seat sat Major Yossi. At twenty-eight, he had come a long way—from Manchuria, in fact. Yossi loved to talk about his origins. It wasn't every Israeli who could boast of being "Chinese." Compact and brown haired, Yossi had been married five years and was the father of two.

Yossi's mind was preoccupied also. He was thinking of his wife Sara. She was trying so hard to be a good army wife in their modest Ashdod apartment, and yet she remained so completely unreconciled to the exigencies of army life. Sara had come from a closely knit family in Jerusalem. Suddenly she found herself on her own in a strange city, bringing up two small children while her husband served in Sinai. And she was apprehensive. Life would be so much easier if Yossi had found civilian employment.

Yossi thought of Sara and smiled. She was lucky that he was an only child and that his parents had refused permission for him to join the paratroopers. Otherwise, Sara would have had more to be worried about.

The driver cursed. A speck of sand had flown into his eye. He wiped it away with a tear and thought of Tel Aviv, of a particular discothèque and a particular girl with green eyes. He also thought of cold grapefruit juice. "This is a dog's life," he murmured to himself as the jeep plowed through the sand ruts.

Yossi began thinking of his unit. Morale was high and so was performance, but tension and fatigue were beginning to take their toll. For the first time in his career, one of his soldiers had recently refused to climb on a tractor. He said that the position was exposed and that he preferred thirty-five days' detention to a cold grave. Yossi had been furious. He climbed on the tractor without another word and began operating the vehicle in full view of the enemy. After a few minutes, the shamefaced soldier pleaded with Yossi to be permitted to continue the work. Yossi smiled. They were good guys. Almost all of them. But what he had done was stupid.

"If I had been killed," he thought, "the tractor driver would have been useless forever. He would never again have driven a vehicle and I would have been dead. I should have convinced him, not shamed him."

The driver manipulated the jeep around a curve in the road. The wall of sand cast a deep shadow across the path. A few hundred meters away, the men could see a bulldozer skittering backwards, apparently a runaway.

"Damn it," yelled the lieutenant, "that machine is completely exposed. Where's the driver? It's a miracle that he hasn't been blown up already."

"Faster," commanded Yossi, thoughts of Sara, of Ashdod, of the difficulties of command quickly evaporated. He preferred action and challenge. It was only during the uncomfortable hiatus between work and sleep that he was really bothered.

Reaching the errant earth mover, Yossi vaulted from the jeep. He instructed the driver and lieutenant to move the vehicle out of the line of fire. Then racing toward the run-away bulldozer and the inert form of Eli on the sand, he heard a familiar sound and froze in his tracks. It was the unmistakable whine of an incoming 82-mm. mortar shell. He turned to cry out and then a fist of hot air sucked him downward.

Yossi staggered toward his companions—one instantly dead, one badly wounded. He tried to focus his eyes but the midday desert had turned into mist.

Elsewhere along the front, the great earth movers continued their relentless work. Steel jaws bit into the sand and heavy reinforced plows carved into the landscape. The curtain of earth was growing higher and more formidable and the fortresses were developing sinew and muscle. Men were moving across the Sinai toward the deadly confrontation with the enemy.

There were a few scattered shots and a lizard scurried across a road seconds before an armored personnel carrier rumbled through. Three new civilian tractor drivers had volunteered for work on the Canal. A helicopter took off. Someone cried and a bulldozer roared into life and bit hard into the lifeless soil of Sinai.

The Suez Canal is Europe's gateway to two vast continents, Africa and Asia. It joins the Mediterranean to the Red Sea, wedding the markets of the West to the Orient, bringing within practical reach all the lands of the Indian and western Pacific Oceans. Men and nations had envisioned a canal through the isthmus many centuries before Ferdinand de Lesseps saw the fruition of the dream in 1859.

Herodotus related that at the end of the sixth century B.C., Pharaoh Necho sacrificed 120,000 diggers in a futile attempt to excavate a path of water between the harsh desert of Sinai and the fertile plains of the Nile. A stone tablet of the fifth century B.C. bears testimony to the efforts of Darius the Great of Persia, conqueror of Egypt, to form a great water trench between the continents. Throughout the centuries, men continued to speculate about a trade route from the Mediterranean to the Red Sea.

The French diplomat de Lesseps, stationed in Egypt, was fevered by this dream. He pored over engineering data, lobbied in the political arena and made countless trips to the trade capitals of the world to gain financial support for the venture. He persevered and witnessed the beginning of one of the most ambitious construction programs in the history of mankind. Over 20,000 Egyptian laborers and more than 4,000 European technicians and engineers had been mobilized for the task. It took ten years for this huge work force to complete the Canal, and the first awesome navigation was accomplished in 1869.

Poor de Lesseps, you think, if he could only see his carefully devised canal today—clogged by stationary boats and crumbling sands, the banks eroding and the seabed rising under the watchful eyes of two armies. From your perch in the observation post, protected by a wall of sandbags, you scan the Canal. Corporal David is on duty. In the darkness his face is almost invisible as you converse quietly.

"How do I see myself? I see myself as a soldier. Most of the time I think of my own particular situation here on the Canal—and it's not a pleasant one although I don't regret that I'm here. But I also think of myself as a representative of the entire State of Israel and so I can't really isolate myself from what's going on elsewhere."

David is twenty and were it not for the vacillations of Moscow and Washington, Jerusalem and Cairo, Paris and Baghdad, the sandy-haired Tel Avivian would be dancing with one of his "four favorite girl friends" or studying for exams at the Technion in Haifa. If he survives the war—and he is confident that he will—he will finish his engineering course. He wants to design airplanes, to marry "any one" of his favorites and to be a father.

"Of course mainly we concern ourselves about our military position and the enemy's, but we don't limit ourselves to the day-to-day situation. We try to understand what we are doing and why we do it.

"Yes, we have lots of problems. On the one hand,

I know we have a good case, and if we behave rationally I believe we can convince other people to understand us. On the other hand, we were victors three years ago and we are no longer the underdog. The world, you know, likes to help the underdog. I think the Arabs are making good use of the situation. They play their parts well and try to make the world forget that they were the ones who attacked us three times. This poses a new dilemma for Jews. We haven't been conquerors since we were expelled from Judea two thousand years ago. Somehow we must manage to get across the idea that we are the attacked and not the attackers. I don't know how this can be done. There are men with more experience than I in the Foreign Office. They get paid for that."

A fish splashes its tail in the water below and a late star appears over the horizon.

"I think world opinion wavers. I know there are many people, even some who are friendly to us, who are more pro-Arab than pro-Israel. It really all depends on circumstances. We mistakenly bomb a military or semi-military factory near Cairo and some Egyptian civilians are killed and world opinion condemns us, even though we apologize. Then the Fatah kills women and children or innocent tourists and the world is suddenly reminded of what Arab terrorism really is. And again world opinion swings in our favor."

"May I say something?" An uncorporeal voice interrupts from further inside the post. "I think it all depends on propaganda. The Arabs are known to be highly skilled."

The Arabs are saying the same thing about the Israelis, you muse.

"I know what you're thinking," continues the voice, "but there's a big difference between Arab propaganda and ours. We tell the truth. The Arabs don't mind lying if it furthers their cause. If you believed the Arabs, there wouldn't be an Israeli soldier left on this line. According to their propagandists, they have destroyed more airplanes than we own."

"Look," David interrupts, "if you're public opinion you're not standing on both sides of the border. Someone in France or Holland doesn't know what really happens if there's a clash, doesn't know who initiated the action. And that's the point because if this person in Holland or France is pro-Arab, he'll believe the Arabs, and if he's pro-Israel, he'll believe us."

For a while the evening seems to drift quietly with the clouds. You remember standing in full sunshine near the Allenby Bridge soon after the Six Day War. A woman and child pass you on the way to self-imposed exile. She is erect and nervous. Halfway across the bridge the boy turns and stares deeply into your eyes with such hatred that his face still haunts you.

"What about the occupied territories?" you ask your companions.

"I don't know what's going on," admits David. "I know only what I read in the papers and what I hear. Of one thing I'm certain, though—the Arabs are getting a much better deal than they would have given us if the situation were reversed and they were sitting in Israel."

"No question about that," the voice agrees. "I don't believe it when a Fatah says he doesn't hate the Jews but only hates the Zionists because I think that practically all Israelis are Zionists—at least 99.9 per cent of us."

"That's right," David confirms. "Israeli Jews are Zionists, so for us it's no comfort at all to hear that they want the Jewish population to remain but don't want any Zionists. The two categories overlap in Israel, whatever the situation may be in other countries."

"I live in Jerusalem," the voice says. "I've seen what is going on in East Jerusalem—what we've built and the way we've tried to bring Jewish and Arab youth together, all that we're doing for the Arab population. If the Arabs had conquered Jerusalem, I'm sure the face of West Jerusalem wouldn't be the same today. I think we're doing as much as we can to help them—in agriculture and in their economy. If they still hate us, then I don't understand them."

The war was won but the war continues. Over three years have passed. What are the hopes for peace, you ask.

"We're sitting here because we have to defend our borders, because we know that if we withdraw, the next defense line is the old border of Israel," David answers. "Better to fight here in Sinai, or on the other side of the Canal, than on the outskirts of Tel Aviv or in Beersheva. One hopes for the best. Basically we are optimistic. Of course, when Egypt says that another war is inevitable, you feel we're not getting anywhere. But everyone hopes in his heart that someday, some solution, some peace will come. I believe that the minute one of the Arab leaders declares he wants peace, we'll agree to it."

"There's something else," adds the voice. "There are people who believe that if we agree to withdraw then the Arabs will change their attitude toward us. On this point I agree completely with our Prime Minister. She said that the problem is not a border. The difficulty is that the Arab nations reject the existence of Israel in any form. Many people tend to forget that between 1948 and 1967 we were content to remain on the old borders. Did the Arabs want peace then? What did they do all those years to make peace?"

But what of the future, you ask. Shall we live forever under the shadow of the Sword of Damocles? Shall we go on sending our children out to fight and die? Shall we continue to gear our economy to the purchase of ammunition and warplanes? Will there never be a quiet border?

"We have much to contribute, if they would let us," David answers. "Israel is a modern, rapidly advancing country, and it can contribute to the progress of the entire area. Provided that we have real peace, of course—not merely a formal treaty but open borders, free traffic among the countries, a movement of tourists, farmers, students and businessmen. I think the whole area can become a sort of federation with each member country contributing its share.

"We can offer our technology, our ideas and culture and can in turn gain from what the other countries have to offer us. It must be an interchange and it's important that people must be free to move within the entire area of the Middle East—the way it used to be, let's say, thirty years ago. I've heard that in those days the joke was 'Yes, Palestine is a nice place to live. In summer you visit your friends in Lebanon and in the winter you spend your time in Egypt.'

"That's the kind of situation we want in serious terms—cooperation in economy, education and agriculture. I know that I'm oversimplifying things, but what

68

could be simpler than the European Common Market? Why should we have visas between neighboring countries? Why can't we have a free flow of merchandise across common borders and tourists crossing as they do throughout Europe? This is what we want here, but of course it depends on what the other side wants too."

"Can I add something?" asks the voice. "My father is a doctor and he travels a great deal. He often meets other doctors who come from Egypt or who have been there and know the problems of Egypt. They still have many chronic diseases, such as cholera and malaria, which were brought under control in Israel a long time ago. If only there was peace, we could do for them what we've done for ourselves."

Yes, if only there was peace, you think, these youngsters, straight out of high school, would be back where they belong, preparing for their futures, instead of trying to wrest some meaning out of the present.

You descend from the observation post, leaving David, the voice, the ever present threat of snipers and the soft wash of Canal waters behind, and make your way to the mess hall. A young, tired lieutenant is drinking coffee. He pours some for you.

Joseph has been at the Canal two months. He was wounded once—lightly, he claims. When he finishes the military, he wants to study. He spends every available moment boning up on mathematics and chemistry. He has a blond girl friend in Tel Aviv who waits for him, but he rarely gets leave. He says that he loves his troops.

"They know what they're doing. They know why they're here. There's no need to encourage them. I never have to threaten or punish or lecture. There's no problem of discipline as there is in other armies. And I don't have to build up their morale. They know what the issues are and they know that the entire State of Israel is behind us.

"We're not playing games here," he says sharply. "The Egyptians are trying to kill us and we're trying to kill them. My job is to save as many Israeli lives as possible.

"We'll not budge unless ordered to. We're fighting a type of war we're not trained for—a static war. Sometimes, particularly when one of my men is hurt, I pray that we'll be given orders to attack. I know we'll pay a terrible price, but you pay a price sitting still as well."

What about the Russians on the other side?

Joseph gets up and pours two more cups of coffee.

"You ask me a question and you deserve an answer," he says as he hands over your cup. "I don't know what they're saying in Jerusalem or what Abba Eban is thinking. I don't even know what Joseph Tekoah is saying at the United Nations. I know only one thing. I hate the Russians and strangely enough I have never hated the Arabs. The Arabs would have made peace a long time ago had it not been for the Russians. I can understand the Arabs facing us. After all, they are only soldiers like us. But they are *miskenim*, unfortunates, because their leaders have misled them and forced them to fight a war which is wrong for them. But the Russians are something else. They are truly evil.

"You know, I have cried only once since my bar mitzvah, and do you know when that was? It was when the Russians invaded Czechoslovakia. I cried, and I'm not ashamed of it. I cried because I couldn't believe that it could happen again. I thought that such things had ended with Hitler. I would have fought the Russians then if there had been some way.

"Let me tell you something. This will not be another Czechoslovakia.

"I'm not naïve. I don't expect that little Israel can withstand all of Russia. I don't believe that the United States will commit troops to help us. Why should they? They have enough troubles of their own. But we'll fight. We'll make them pay dearly. We'll die but they will die too. The Russians still think that we are the ghetto Jews that their Cossacks used to beat with lead-tipped whips. They'll learn that there's been a change since then."

Joseph's face pulses with anger. "I'm sorry about the lecture," he says, "and for losing my temper. I guess I'm a little tired and you hit a nerve."

The Desert

A great burst of cold descends and wraps your trembling body in misery. You burrow into the thin fabric of a sleeping bag but your muscles shake uncontrollably as the desert wind performs strange tricks. Once you were foolish enough to believe that a desert is a furnace of white heat. Now you know differently; your gums numb and your teeth begin to chatter. You shift your gaze from a pearl-white disk suspended in a void 286,000 miles away to the dying embers of a fire. You think of a tribe of Semitic nomads wandering for forty years in this strange wasteland called Sinai.

Earlier in the day, before the sun was up, you had wearily struggled to the windy summit of Jebel Musa, the lonely pinnacle 7,482 feet high, where, according to Greek Orthodox tradition, Moses received the stone birthright for the children of Israel. You climbed until your muscles ached, and then when you thought you had reached the top, you discovered a seemingly endless ladder of roughly hewn steps. Finally on top, you slumped against a stone structure and tried to draw the faint sunlight into your body. The wind was your only companion in this awesome wilderness of stone mountains towering to the clouds.

What kind of enigma is this Sinai, bleached white

by the sun and atrophied by the cold, where small islands of green date palms and bushes dot the great carpets of sand, where the Mediterranean laps the white beaches of El Arish and the Red Sea foams over layers of coral and exotic sea life?

Standing on the pinnacle of Jebel Musa—also known as Mount Sinai or Har Moshe—you, an Israeli, feel no particular affinity toward this massive fist of stone and sand called Sinai which is three and one-half times larger than all of Israel. Your ancestors had wandered here, but so had a thousand other tribes plying the caravan paths between ancient Egypt and Mesopotamia. There had been Roman legions and Hellenes. There were the sons of Ham who had sailed their dhows up from East Africa. There were the moving tribes of Araby, and Ottomans and British colonials and Egyptian troops. There were Israelis in 1956 and again in 1967. But no one owns Sinai, you reflect, no one could own Sinai except the Bedouins.

Unlike the others the Bedouins have always been in Sinai and they will always be there. They do not intrude on the landscape. They melt into it. They are like drops of water fertilizing the parched soil. They appear out of nowhere and are oftentimes the only testimony to life in the solitary landscape.

How many Bedouins are there in Sinai? No one really knows. Estimates range between 12,000 and 30,000 souls of a wide and dissimilar family of tribes, one often hostile to the other. The Jebaliya, the people of the mountain, originated in Constanza and were imported to protect the area in the eighth century, and are now the devoutly Moslem caretakers of Santa Caterina monastery.

The Azazmeh are the largest tribe on the peninsula, with suzerainty over large tracts in central and northern Sinai. There are also the Tarabin of central Sinai, the Grarshe of the southwest and the friendly Muzeinah tribe who believe that, in a moment of peril, Allah will lift them by their hair directly into Paradise.

The Bedouin moves and evolves and changes at a pace regulated by his environment. He is not conscious of the passage of time. When did the event occur? A long time ago. How long ago? A long time ago! When were you born? Once, many years before! Many years before what? A shrug. Time is calibrated on a different instrument, on a tape measure formed of a hundred miles of sand, of full moons and sudden cloudbursts and the birth of livestock.

"*Kif el jamal*? How is your camel?" begins the Bedouin conversation. "*Kif el ranam*? How is your sheep?" he pursues the matter further. These are the important mainstays. The rest is peripheral. There is an ever present need for water, and the oasis is the key to his existence. The sun-warmed streams sustain his flocks, and his flocks sustain him. His family is chattel. His wives and his numberless children are recorded with his other few possessions—his loose-fitting *abbaya*, his *khaffiya* which protects his head and face from the midday sun and evening frost, his curved *Jabriya* knife, his goatskin canteen, his hand-me-down overcoat and plastic sandals left over from previous desert skirmishes, his rifle and his transistor.

The latter is the key to the Sinai Bedouin's present situation. In 1956, when Israeli armor stormed across the desert wastelands, the impact on the Bedouin was negligible. The northern intruder made little impression on the indigenous population, fundamentally apolitical and owing allegiance only to tribe and family.

One day there had been the foreign troops of Nasser and the next day there were the foreign forces of Ben Gurion. Both armies were strangers to the landscape. The Egyptians were a race of *fellahin*—peasants—an object of derision to every Arab nomad, and although they spoke Arabic and prayed to Allah, their religion was not the same and their dialect almost unintelligible. The Jew was even more strange—his language, his looks, his behavior, but both Jew and Arab were passively accepted by the Bedouin who has seen many strange things.

What was important was that both intruders should adhere to the rules of the desert—that they should not tamper with the Bedouins' religion, their water or their women, that they should pay oil, salt and flour to the sheikhs, the custodians of the land, as a guarantee to free passage and safety. These had been the rules for a thousand years.

And then came the era of the transistor.

In early June 1967, every Bedouin knew that the two armies were poised to strike. Northern Sinai had been turned into a vast Egyptian armory. On June 5, Radio Cairo announced the dawn of war and promised an easy and decisive victory to be celebrated in Tel Aviv. Throughout the day the Bedouins heard of Egyptian victories on all fronts, of lightning thrusts toward Ashkelon, of the pillar of flames that once was Haifa, of the virtual capture of Beersheva. Then they tuned in on the Arabic newscasts of Radio Israel. They heard claims of a stunning defeat of Egyptian armor and air power. They heard that the Israeli forces had penetrated into the Gaza Strip and were fanning out throughout Sinai. They heard and waited.

When Israeli tanks cut through the peninsula and Egyptian forces cast away their arms and fled toward Kantara and Mitla, the Bedouin tuned in to pronouncements of victory from Cairo. And when Israeli aircraft swept the Sinai skies, Radio Cairo claimed even more spectacular victories. The Bedouin observed the mutilation of the army of the Nile while listening to reports that Nasser had annihilated the Zionists. His sense of credibility was strained. Although impartial to the outcome, he knew a lie even in the most flowery of languages. So the transistor disabused him of Egyptian propaganda, probably for a long time to come.

Is he happy with the Israeli occupation? The question is not germane. More important, ask him if he is getting his flour, salt and oil; if his wells are functioning; if his flocks are flourishing.

Israel is no stranger to handling Bedouins. The tribes range through Israel from the southern Negev to the northern Galilee. Some tribes remain isolated and supplement their meager existence by drug traffic and the sale of military information. Others have become friendly, and some have even folded their tents and created small desert settlements near permanent water facilities. One Bedouin has earned a medical degree from the Hebrew University in Jerusalem, and several Bedouin tribes take pride in the fact that their sons serve in the Israeli army. They are superb fighters, but one must pity the Bedouin soldier who is captured alive

79

by Arabs. He dies slowly.

From the point of view of acquiring an alien indigenous population, the occupation of Sinai poses almost no problems. The local population is small and spread over a vast area. Allegiances are tribal, not national, and it is a rare tribesman who laments for the Egyptian fellah. The problem of maintaining an internal peace is small, and the geographical and tactical advantages are enormous.

These are your thoughts as you crouch in your sleeping bag, enveloped by the Sinai cold. You suddenly sense that you are not alone and that eyes are watching you. You ease the safety off your Parabellum and point in the direction of a shadow.

Amiram, your companion and guide, springs to his feet. Like a cat, he rises in one swift motion, a Kalachnikov automatic rifle in his hands.

"*Kif Inti?*" a voice calls out.

"*El Hamdulillah,*" answers Amiram, his rifle still trained at our guest.

The Bedouin points to a pack of cigarettes near the smoldering fire. Amiram hands him the pack. The Bedouin smiles and his teeth are brilliantly white in the moonlight. He unslings his rifle, crouches near the fire and stares curiously at us. He finishes his cigarette and pantomimes for another. Amiram divides the pack in half. The Bedouin smiles again, rises slowly and backs off into the night. The sand swallows him effortlessly.

You cannot begin to think of the Israeli fighting man in Sinai without thinking of Amiram—a citizen-soldier of conspicuous individuality, a special type of man born of the land and the army. Slight of build and edging forty,

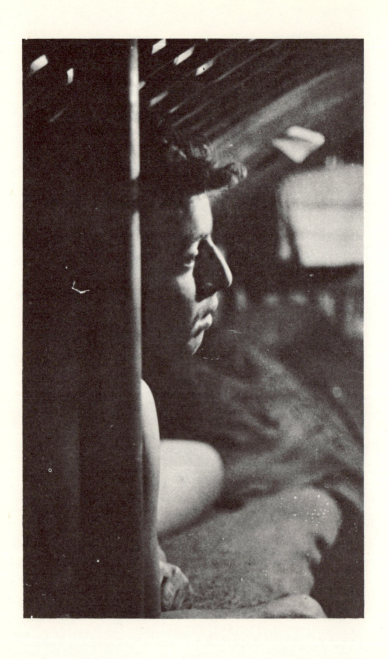

he looks like an older version of Huckleberry Finn. He is a third-generation Sabra who believes that nothing is impossible "if you do your homework properly and define your objectives precisely."

Amiram belongs to the generation of Sabras who became dedicated "desert rats." From army positions in the red mountains of Judah, they grew accustomed to the harsh beauty of the desert. An officer in Zahal, Amiram drove a specially tailored jeep through the desert sands, searching for infiltrators from Jordan. Slicing through unexplored caverns and sand pits, he and his men trapped and caught them in their seemingly invulnerable desert strongholds.

During that brief period in 1956 when Israel controlled Sinai, Amiram grew infatuated with the new land. He began charting the wadis and mountain paths for future reference.

By the time Sinai was returned to Egypt, he was back at his civilian occupation as a consultant for the Ministry of Agriculture in the Negev. The desert still intrigued him. "The Negev represents half of Israel," the sandy-haired farmer says, "and everyone from Ben Gurion down was clamoring for settlement and cultivation. And yet— despite all the words and all the appeals—almost nothing had been done. There were a few isolated *kibbutzim*, but on the scale required, they represented almost nothing."

Amiram had a dream and its color was green. He believed that despite the fiendish heat, the denuded landscape, the salinity of the available water, life could flourish in the Negev. And if life could be coaxed from the soil, then settlements could be sustained and the Negev could become the heritage of future generations.

"We selected the site of Neot Hakikar—which means the square plain—because there was Biblical evidence that there had once been settlements on the southern fringe of the Dead Sea," he explains. "British agricultural experts had claimed that the salinity level of the available water in the area was two and a half times greater than could sustain any form of agriculture. Maybe that's why, according to the Bible, the land was cursed."

Receiving virtually no official help, Amiram and several other "believers" employed by the Ministry of Agriculture resigned and began scraping away at the salt-encrusted earth with primitive tools. They would have starved had not workers in the nearby Dead Sea Potash Works agreed to consign their leftover lunches to the small group. All this started in 1958, and over a period of years the landscape was gradually altered. Date palms began to flourish. Winter tomatoes, onions and peppers were grown. Cattle were brought in from Rhodesia. A profitable settlement was established near the site of ancient Sodom.

"By 1961 we had proved the point, but the Negev remained the same challenge. We had acquired a considerable amount of experience in the army exploring the wadis and mountains of the Negev. It occurred to us that this could be turned into a useful tourist commodity. We acquired some war-surplus command cars, modified them for our purpose and began providing regular desert tours."

Before the embers of war had cooled in 1967, Amiram was already busy on Sinai desert ventures.

"Sinai represents the greatest challenge Israel has ever faced," he contends. "Wadi El Arish is fertile and can sustain considerable settlement. The Dahab oasis is one of the most intriguing in the world. In fact, the entire peninsula provides a marvelous climate for a special kind of rugged tourism."

And so you lie in the winter desert, curled into your sleeping bag, speculating about your friend's dream, while shells and mortars are falling between Kantara in the north and Suez in the south. The Jewish people are inextricably wed to the desert, you think, this desert— the wilderness of Sinai—and the Negev with its rolling, sandy Arava plain and bared, ribbed mountains. You were a desert wanderer in the time of Abraham, no less a Bedouin than the Jebaliya or the Muzeinah. You originated from a warrior clan long years before the suffocating pressures of Roman slavery and European ghettoism turned you into a merchant and money changer. There is something splendidly atavistic about your being where you are now. The desert is your legacy.

You recall a discussion among top officials right after the Six Day War on the problems of the occupied areas: the West Bank with its large population of shocked, restive Arabs; the Gaza Strip, an artificial appendage fed on fanatical hatred for the last generation; the Golan Heights, tactically indispensable but presenting some ethnic problems. In contrast, the advantages of Sinai seem so obvious to you that even the enervating wind cannot conceal them. You count the blessings: Sinai provides an early-warning buffer against the well-equipped Egyptian air force. It ensures freedom of navigation through the Straits of Tiran. It creates a natural tank arena between Cairo and Tel Aviv. It supplies Israel with advanced bases. It adds the Israeli presence to the Suez Canal. It poses no

85

difficulties with the local population. It opens up vistas for the eventual resettlement of large segments of the Palestine refugees.

You recall a document, almost haunting in its prescience, which referred to Sinai. More than fifty years ago the man who was Chief of Intelligence to General Allenby in Palestine, R. Meinertzhagen, wrote to the Prime Minister of England, Lloyd George, a thoughtful and almost too accurate analysis of the sovereignty of Sinai.

In his letter, with uncanny foresight, he warned the Prime Minister:

> This peace conference [Versailles] has laid two eggs— Jewish nationalism and Arab nationalism; these are going to grow up into troublesome chickens. . . . In fifty years time, both Jew and Arab will be obsessed by nationalism, the natural outcome of the President's [Wilson] self-determination. Nationalism prefers self-government, however dishonest and inefficient, to government by foreigners, however efficient and beneficial. Nationalism moreover involves the freedom of the state but ignores the freedom of the individual; it is a sop to professional politicians and agitators, and may involve gross injustice to the people.
>
> A national home for the Jew must develop sooner or later into sovereignty; I understand that this natural evolution is envisaged by some members of His Majesty's Government. Arab nationalism will also develop into sovereignty from Mesopotamia to Morocco.
>
> Jewish and Arab sovereignty must clash. The Jew,

86

if his immigration programme succeeds, must expand, and that can only be accomplished at the expense of the Arab who will do his utmost to check the growth and power of a Jewish Palestine. That means bloodshed. . . .

I now come to Palestine's position vis-à-vis Egypt. The Egyptians, even with superior numbers, are no match for an inferior Jewish army. But as modern weapons—tanks and aircraft—develop, offensive power rests more and more on human bravery and endurance. That is why I regard Egypt as Palestine's potential enemy.

With Jewish and Arab nationalism developing into sovereignty and with the loss of the Canal in 1966 (only 47 years hence), we [England] stand a good chance of losing our position in the Middle East. My suggestion to you . . . is a proposal to make our position in the Middle East more secure. . . . General Allenby, with British forces, unaided by the Egyptian army, conquered and occupied Turkish Sinai which, by right of conquest, is at Britain's disposal. This bare statement can be verified by the Foreign Office.

If Britain annexes Turkish Sinai, the following advantages accrue:

1. It establishes a buffer between Egypt and Palestine.
2. It gives Britain a strong foothold in the Middle East with access to both the Mediterranean and the Red Sea.
3. It gives us room for a strategic base and, *with Jewish consent,* the best harbour in the eastern

Mediterranean.

4. It not only places us in a position whence we can frustrate any Egyptian move to close the Canal to British shipping, but it enables us to build a dual canal connecting the Mediterranean with the Red Sea.
5. No question of nationalism can arise in Sinai, as its nomad inhabitants are but a few thousand.

Skies Over Sinai

You touch the machine-gunned fuselage of what was once a Mig fighter, somewhere in Sinai, and you close your eyes and imagine a bright morning, three years earlier, when delta-winged darts brushed the sand surface of Sinai at incredible speeds and a few hours later paralyzed Nasser's dream of military victory.

"It is sad," says red-headed Capt. Yigal, a compact fighter pilot who stands in your shadow and kicks the blackened earth where the plane was scorched.

"Why don't you remove it?" you ask.

Yigal shrugs. "I don't know. Perhaps it is meant to be a monument to something. Perhaps the plane remains there so that we shouldn't forget that the threat of war is still with us."

Overhead a squadron of Mirages pass by. The ground seems to vibrate.

Yigal is 23 years old. He is married and he has an infant daughter. He has spent all his life in a kibbutz and when his Air Force service is over, he will return to the kibbutz. He never talks about his exploits, but you have been told he has shot down two Egyptian aircraft.

You take a hard look at Yigal. He is so confident about the prowess of the Israel Air Force, of the invulnerability of the Israeli State, that you wonder what kind of alchemistry occurred in slightly more than two decades to produce such human material. Unassuming, bashful Yigal could be the prototype for all Israeli pilots. He is totally dedicated and totally convinced. You imagine that he has his fears and his complexities, that there are unrequited ambitions and frustrations but he has learned to master them. And for a pilot, he retains another decided advantage—he loves the air; he feels totally at home in the skies.

The skies over Sinai are traditionally cloudless, bright and clear, and today is no exception. The only two disturbing anomalies occur when the overflow of the nearby Nile causes an occasional spate of puffy clouds and when swift, darting metal shapes crash through the still air at supersonic speeds bending sound around the armed furrows that inundate both sides of the Suez Canal.

Sandy swaths of the Sinai Peninsula were the graveyard of Egyptian military ambitions. In five hours, on June 5, 1967, the largest air force in the Middle East, replete with Mig 21s, TU-16s and MI-6 helicopters was turned into a shambles of burned out fuselages and assorted wreckage. There has been no similar instance in history whereby an armed force had been so totally and decisively obliterated in a time span calibrated in minutes. There were 609 Egyptian war planes in the Cairo inventory before the war. By the time the war ended, 386 were destroyed. Since then nearly 100 others have been destroyed by Israeli ground fire and in air combat.

The Israeli air action set the tone for the entire

six-day campaign. Denuded of its air strength, Egyptian armor was stripped open by rockets and napalm. The epilogue was written at the Mitla Pass where hundreds of tanks and assorted military vehicles were caught in a man-made *cul-de-sac* and relentlessly hammered into destruction and surrender.

The Six Day War merely confirmed what every Israeli accepts as a fundamental axiom to his continued existence—the skies of the Middle East must be dominated by the planes marked with the star of the House of David. There can be no compromising on that point. The alternative would be national suicide.

The point of the defeat was not lost on Egypt, Israel's only serious adversary in the Middle East power struggle. Had the Israeli air attack faltered, had Egypt been better prepared, had a heavy toll been taken of attacking Israeli Mirage III's, Vautours, Ouragons, Magisters and Mysteres, then the situation might have been a very different one. The Egyptian ground forces might not have buckled so completely and in such short order. Air reprisals might have kept the Israeli Air Force at bay.

Valuable time might have been won—time which could have saved King Hussein from the near total humiliation of losing not only East Jerusalem but all of the West Bank. A fighting, united Arab front, albeit a defensive one, would have prevented the all-out Israeli offensive against the Syrian forces on the Golan Heights.

The overall outcome of the war may not have been too different but the ultimate losses and subsequent military consequences might have been substantially mitigated—might have been that is if the Israelis had not

93

so totally dominated the skies. But "might" is a euphemism which had been elusive in this part of the world long years before Richard the Lion Hearted was bested by Saladin. The "might equations" in the Middle East are legendary. What "might" have happened had not Titus . . . what "might" have happened had not Hitler . . . what "might" have happened in 1948 had the Arabs. . . .

Within two weeks of the conclusion of the Six Day War, however, the Soviet Union, that most persistent of all arms suppliers, began an airlift that can be compared in effectiveness only to the American airlift of blockaded West Berlin. Crated Mig replacements began arriving with an intensity that amazed the military pundits both in Washington and Jerusalem. Russia had invested heavily in Nasser. It had poured about $1.5 billion into the Egyptian arsenal. Not only was Russian prestige at stake but its very foothold in the Middle East was jeopardized by Israel's decisive victory. The choice was either to cut losses and go or resupply and stay. The Kremlin opted for the latter. In short order, 325 modern replacement aircraft were delivered and the Egyptian Air Force was soon stronger than ever before. Older Migs were replaced by the latest Mig 21s and Sukhoi 7s attack aircraft and a covenant was signed between the two powers calling for immediate replacement of any aircraft destroyed in combat or through accidents.

Since nearly all the Egyptian aircraft were caught on the ground, the problem was equipment and not trained personnel. And equipment was a commodity which Russia was prepared to lavish.

By the end of 1968, the Egyptian Air Force, numbered about 400 frontline aircraft and the overall structure of the air arm was revised by the Soviet advisers.

The presence of new Sukhoi 7s and late-model Mig 21s began to be felt. A profusion of SAM missile bases mushroomed along the western bank of the Canal and were located in every conceivable strategic area near military and industrial sites. Russian advisers and technicians began arriving with alarming regularity and the number of these "volunteers" was estimated in April 1970 at well over 7,000. The Russians demanded and obtained a say in Air Force training. They insisted upon more air exercises. Large numbers of Egyptian pilots were ferried to the Soviet Union and eastern satellite countries for more intensive preparations.

The Six Day War had been a catastrophe for the Soviet Union. It could not be permitted to happen again. Otherwise, Russia would not only lose its investment, its precious foothold on the Mediterranean, it could face some alarming problems at home. There had already been enough cause for a thorough post-mortem about the costs involved and the sacrifice of civilian commodity items on the altar of Arabic socialism. Over $3 billion had been poured into Egypt in a perilously short period. Egypt was becoming the Kremlin's Vietnam.

Interestingly, during the twilight period between the conclusion of the war and the heating up around the Canal, Israel's major difficulty arose not in the air but in the political arenas of Paris. Its most steadfast supplier had turned into a bitter, oftentimes acrimonious, adversary. First De Gaulle and then Pompidou. The words changed, but the tune remained the same.

France would no longer supply Israel with aircraft. Fifty Mirage V attack planes lay mothballed at the

95

Dassault factory. For a time even Mirage III replacement parts were banned. A victorious Israel had won a decisive war only to see the fruit turn sour. The Egyptian Air Force was growing stronger and more threatening every day but the Israeli purchasing mission was paralyzed.

The Israel Air Force was facing yet another Soviet-originated problem. The other Arab air forces were rising like phoenixes from the Six Day War defeat and imposing an ever more serious logistics problem on the IAF.

In short order, Algeria received 223 planes, nine more than it had before the Six Day War. Iraq received 308 warplanes—134 since the cease-fire. Syria lost 77 aircraft during the Six Day War and received 160 modern replacements. Jordan, Saudi Arabia and Lebanon began procuring aircraft from the West and Libya signed a massive arms agreement pact with France calling for the delivery of over 100 Mirages. And the aircraft shipments, particularly from the Soviet Union, continue up to this very moment.

What Pompidou was unwilling to provide, despite the vociferous objections of Marcel Dassault and two thirds of the French citizenry polled on the subject, the United States was prepared to sell to Israel for her defense.

Israel began retiring some of its older vintage aircraft from France and replacing them with A-4 Skyhawks. In the hands of competent Israeli pilots they were soon to prove the scourge of Arab military emplacements in Egypt and Jordan.

Cut off from its supply of Mirages, Israel chose the F-4 Phantom and placed an urgent order for 50 of these modern fighter-bombers which had proved themselves

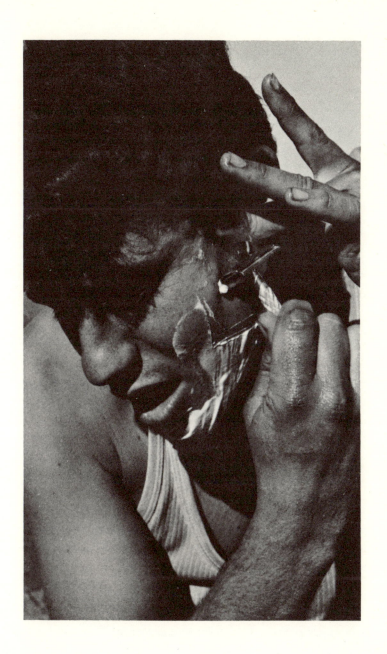

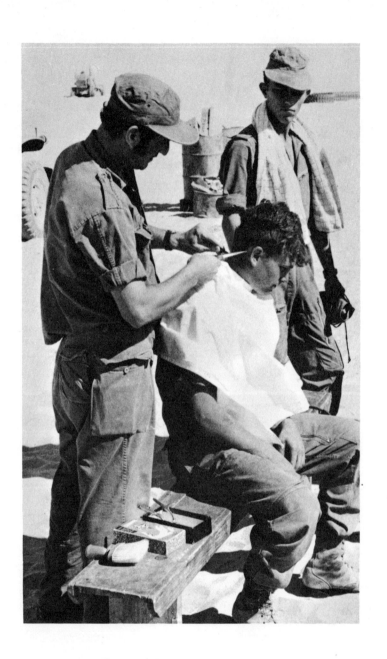

so ably in the skies over Southeast Asia.

For both Israel and Egypt, the arrival of the Phantoms opened up a Pandora's Box of new problems and escalations. Economically-hurting Israel had to pay $4.5 million for each of the McDonnell-Douglas planes— three times more than it cost to acquire a Mirage III. This triggered a spate of budgetary difficulties and new taxes in a country which was hobbled by incredible financial undertakings. The Israeli war machine already devoured most of the country's economic resources. Immigration to Israel, a most welcome phenomenon in an area where 2.5 million Jews are surrounded by 100 million Arabs calling for a Jihad, required enormous expenditures and capital. And to top it off, luxury-craving Israelis were in the midst of a monumental buying spree which was draining the country's foreign currency reserves at a catastrophic rate.

As far as Egypt was concerned, the delivery of the Phantoms and the promise of more to come meant that an aggressive enemy would be equipped with aggressive machinery. Using Sinai bases and with a Phantom combat radius of 1000 kms., Egypt became untenably vulnerable. Israeli planes darkened the skies south and southwest of Cairo. There was nothing useful in all of Egypt that could not be crippled by the fiercely manned Phantoms. Having lived through the Six Day War, Nasser's nervousness was not only evident but understandable, when Israeli aircraft swooped over Helwan.

The stage for the eventual air confrontation was set in 1968. When Egypt felt strong enough and the frustrations emanating from its losses had reached a high-water mark, the static defense situation was converted into a limited offensive campaign. The Nile strategy was simple. Israel must not be permitted to feel too comfortable in its new perch. The world must not forget that Sinai is an integral part of Egypt. The hurting Arab masses must be bolstered and encouraged. The United Nations must be forced into action. The result was a fierce slugging match of artillery with limited Israeli air action to keep the rapidly expanding Egyptian army from consolidating its forces for an offensive punch.

By 1969, the Suez situation had reached a sort of limited blood-letting modus vivendi. Both sides were occasionally hurt by surprise shells and the world headlines attested to the intransigence of the situation which had surprisingly been kept under reasonable control.

A new dimension was soon added, however, when Nasser was accused by fellow Arab rulers of defeatism and military lethargy. Soviet political pressure had failed to unseat the Israelis. The army of the Nile was brimming with armament and Arab mercurialism demanded, and finally got, a dose of new pepper. Egypt opened up with everything it had on the Canal. Specially trained commandos were sent across on nocturnal ambush and sabotage missions. Israeli losses began to mount.

At the same time, the Arab guerrilla organizations intensified widespread terror activities against Israel. The convenient Lebanese border was turned into a training camp for the Palestinians. The entire length of the Jordan border erupted in nocturnal warfare. The Beit Sha'an kibbutzim were relentlessly hammered by Katyusha rockets. El Al, the Israeli flag carrier, was especially marked by the Palestine Liberation Front and its planes were attacked in the air and on the ground.

The problem was that for both political and military reasons Israel was not interested in forging deeper into Arab lines. The losses would have been catastrophic and the gains negligible. And even if Israel won, what possible advantage could be obtained by adding Amman and Cairo to its list of victories? The presence of more millions of Arab refugees and captives would only worsen an already exacerbated situation. And then what of the United Nations? What of the Soviet Union? What would the free world say?

Thus Israel opted for limited ground reprisals in the form of lightning commando raids such as the capture of Shadwan Island located right in the Gulf of Suez. Israel still maintained mastery over the air. Egypt would learn to rue its decision to escalate.

An entire radar unit was captured. Israeli ambushes turned the west bank of the Canal into an Egyptian nightmare. According to western reports, a Sukhoi 7 was added to the Israeli collection of Migs. Nasser was to be embarrassed. But embarrassment does not win wars and the vital key to Israeli counteraction lay in the air.

Israel would reply with Skyhawks to Nasser's war of attrition. Later it would call on its new Phantoms.

Before the planes could begin hammering at Egypt, however, they had to pass through an infiltration zone provided by Soviet SAM's. In Yigal's inimitible explanation Israel had to "block out SAM's by destroying SAM's radar," thus blinding the missile bases.

Hence, in mid-1969, Israeli airplanes began a concerted and well planned effort to punch holes through the Egypt's Soviet-supplied missile net.

During the initial air actions, the Egyptians relied on the mesh of radar-controlled antiaircraft guns and missile batteries. On the rare occasions when Mig fighters appeared, they were either downed or forced to turn tail.

Working stolidly, Israeli fighters began a series of attacks which soon built up in relentlessness and fury. Dozens of sorties were flown each week, and to no one's amazement, the SAM sites proved ineffective against the attackers.

By early 1970, the missile net had been effectively shredded and Israeli aircraft were free to roam to the very suburbs of Cairo. The border was now on Cairene hotels and administrative offices

The Egyptian Air Force reacted. Air resistance against the attackers was offered in a spotty fashion. At the same time, Migs and Sukhois began hit-and-run operations against stationary Israeli targets on the east bank. Egyptian successes against the Israeli fortresses were negligible but occasional forays produced the desired number of casualties.

In comparison with the organized Israeli air attacks, the Egyptian efforts were feeble. The Egyptian forces were under a cloud of air attack and the cloud was moving closer to the very heart of Egypt. Rooftop spectators in Cairo saw Israeli warplanes range too close for comfort.

Nasser had begun a war of attrition and despite massive quantitative superiority, his war was turning sour on him. The Egyptian frontline was turned into a shambles and the "coming Arab victory" was for the fourth time in a generation converted into smoldering ashes.

Then the Soviet Union played its trump card. More Russian planes than ever were delivered. The SAM-2 missile sites were augmented by the ultra-modern SAM-3 installations which were to provide effective low-level cover against attacking planes. The army of Russian "advisers" stationed in Egypt began to swell. They and they alone were to man and protect the top-secret SAM-3 installations. It would be tantamount to disaster should Israel succeed in hijacking one of the new stations. Russian officers filtered down into command positions along the front. And then the Sunday punch! Russian airmen were to guard the Egyptian skies over Aswan, Helwan, Cairo and Alexandria. Soviet pilots were to release Egyptian pilots for attack missions.

By late summer, three Soviet-piloted Migs were reported downed by Israeli airmen. The Russian air commander immediately flew to Cairo for emergency consultations. In the meantime, the delivery of SAMs reached a frenetic level. New missile batteries were erected throughout the front—many on a staggered system and their presence finally succeeded in introducing a new dimension to the ground-to-air war. Israeli planes began falling like wounded eagles.

"Yigal," you ask, "does it bother you, the fact that one day you may find yourself in an aerial confrontation with a Russian?" "It doesn't bother me at all," he answers. "I don't think anyone wants a war with Russia, but that really doesn't depend on us. Does it? The presence of the Russian pilots has already limited us but I think the lines have already been drawn. As long as Nasser pro-claims war on the Canal and backs it up with artillery bombardments and commando attacks, we have no

103

choice but to keep hitting them along the front.

"You have to understand the strategic implications. The Egyptians are far too strong for us to allow them to build up their forces for an all-out attack. Think for a moment about the choices! If we allow them to maintain the offensive, then our losses will become insufferable. If we withdraw to a new line, then they will take back the Canal and establish a new base closer to Israel."

Soviet Shadows on the Sands of Time

You have not forgotten the impassioned support the fledgling Jewish State received from the two major power blocs emerging from World War II, the U.S. and the Soviet Union. And you recall the solid help the Jews got from them during Israel's war for survival.

Grimly, you think that Soviet troops are facing you across the Canal, that more than 10,000 Russian "advisers" are providing the military ante for Egypt's latest desperate gamble, that the communist high command has ordered protective sorties to be flown by airmen from Odessa and Kiev, and that those are Red Army personnel guarding Russian antiaircraft rockets, that Alexandria and Port Said have become Soviet ports in the Mediterranean, that upward of seventy Soviet warships are permanently scurrying across the Middle Sea—from the "Boiky" and "Gnewny" rocket-firing destroyer class to the 20,000-ton "Moscva" with its thirty-six helicopters and marine commando contingents.

You have never seen Ivan, hidden 100 yards away on the Egyptian side of the Canal. You know he is there and you know that he knows that you are here. You cannot help thinking how odd it is that you are crouched almost within talking distance of each other—stranger for him because he is now in a thoroughly alien environment, far from Mother Russia.

An Egyptian automatic weapon begins coughing. The gun sounds as if it is gargling in sand. Someone on the other side has leaned too heavily on the trigger of his Kalachnikov and the weapon clears its steel throat with hot lead which pricks the gray embankment of the east bank of Suez.

In the bunker defenses, you span the centuries between the tenth, when Oleg from Kiev planted his banner on the shores of the Bosporus, and the twentieth, when Nasser became beholden to the Kremlin.

You recall how serious Soviet penetration of the Middle East began after the Sinai War in 1956. Having a stake in the Aswan Dam, Russia agreed to reforge the broken Egyptian army with Soviet steel. The shadow of the hammer and sickle was long from Syria and Iraq in the east to Algeria in the west. In one decade, between 1955 and 1965, Russia poured $3 billion in economic aid into the area.

You know only too well that the figures tell the story.

On the eve of the Six Day War, there were already more than 1,500 Russian advisers in the United Arab Republic, Iraq and Syria. The military equipment of the Arab countries had been completely converted to products of the East Bloc. The standard tanks were the T-34s, T-54s and T-55s. The regular aircraft line was the Mig, the Sukhoi, the Tupolev, the Ilyushin. The financial investment was high but reasonable in terms of ultimate objectives. By 1964, Russia had gained a naval berth in the Middle East. There were almost no Russian casualties as against the U.S. Vietnam involvement.

Yes, you remind yourself, the great Russian break-through really occurred after the Six Day War. The Soviet web grew tauter in Syria and Iraq. The SAM-2 missile network was established around principal Arab forti-fications. Arab pilots were frenetically ferried to the East Bloc for training. By 1968 the Soviet Mediterranean fleet had grown to forty-five vessels, and these included rocket-firing cruisers of the "Grozny" class.

Russian pilots are now flying combat missions. Amphibious Soviet equipment has reached Suez via Cairo. The super-secret SAM-3, low altitude, antiaircraft missiles are installed all along the Canal.

Past history, present anxieties are interrupted by a new sound—a vehicle speeding into the confines of the fortress. It roars past the barbed wire entanglement and screeches to an abrupt stop. A tiny elf of a man with a steel-gray beard literally flings himself out of the truck and begins cursing. He points to a jagged hole near the radiator. "The bastards nearly did me in," he fumes. "They have the whole road under surveillance."

Someone hands him a cup of coffee and two waffles.

The driver points to the hole again. "This is a rotten way to treat a grandfather." He pulls out a billfold and flashes pictures of two small children dressed in Purim costumes. "They both look just like me," he beams. "If I can dig the shrapnel out of this truck, I will bring it back as a souvenir for the kids."

You note an interesting, perhaps almost unique, characteristic of Zahal. The Israeli army is a people's army in the fullest sense of the word. With few exceptions, every male completes his three years' compulsory military duty and then performs up to two months' annual reserve duty until the age of fifty-five. In most cases, the oldsters are "pensioned off" to civil defense duties by the time they pass through their mid-forties, but there are some, either because of specialized skills or because of personal lobbying, who continue to perform combat missions right up until the end. In many cases, military duty doesn't even end at fifty-five—there is a relatively new organization of men and women in their sixties who volunteer to perform guard duty at the border settlements.

The army is not only an amalgamation of young and old, men and women. It is also ethnically heterogeneous. At least half the country consists of Jews who originated from Eastern or Sephardic cultures, and the Israeli army reflects this composition exactly. Indeed, you remember that before the Six Day War there were those (yourself included) who had misgivings about the morale of an army recruited from discothèque youth and disenchanted youngsters from Sephardic families who felt that the cards were stacked against them. Yet, during the six days of June when the chips were down, the grandsons of Poland and of Iraq fought together and won together. In that sense, the war had a salutary influence on the social fabric of Israel.

"My wife says that I am *meshugah*," says the driver. "She thinks that I should be fishing or sunbathing instead of driving a truck in Sinai. You know, sometimes I think that she is right.

"I have been through more wars than I like to think about. I was in World War II with the British Forces in North Africa and Italy. I served in the War of Liberation and I was wounded in Jerusalem. I was in Sinai during the

1956 campaign and sprained my back (my wife says I sprained my head also) when my truck turned over. In 1967, I had to pull all sorts of strings, but I was back in Sinai; and now here I am again. Maybe I really am *meshugah*."

You ask the grandfather what he does when he is not tooling around with an army vehicle in the desert.

"I have my own accounting firm in Tel Aviv. I have sixteen people working for me. Every time I go into the army, my business goes to hell."

A young mechanic looks at the damaged vehicle. "It will take about an hour to fix it, grandpa," he says.

"So stop talking and do something," the driver snaps, "and don't call me 'grandpa.' I have enough vinegar in me to take care of three like you with my hands tied behind my back."

You ask the driver how long he has been serving on the present stint.

"Sixteen days so far," he replies, "and my nose is so clogged with sand, I can't breathe. If I don't get a bath soon, my skin is going to walk away. My stomach also hurts me. I think I have waffle poisoning. This is some army."

You ask the bearded driver why he volunteered for Sinai. After all, four wars should be enough for any one man.

His elf's-eyes twinkle.

"Lots of reasons, although you are too young to understand most of them. First of all, I don't want to grow old and soft and there is nothing like motoring through the Sinai to keep your balls in condition. Next, I get bored easily. I make my money from a desk but I develop callouses on the arse if I don't do something constructive every so often. Thirdly, I willed this country on my grandchildren. Before they throw sand in my face, I want to be damn certain that I did everything possible in this God-forsaken country of ours. Fourth, my son was gunned down not far from here during the '67 war. Being here, I feel a lot closer to him, although he is buried outside Tel Aviv. So maybe I am not only a little bit crazy, I am also a little bit sentimental. And last of all, I just like being here—so long as nosy people don't ask me too many questions and young twerps don't call me 'grandpa.'"

The driver leaves you in order to inspect the repair work on the vehicle. "Where did you learn to fix trucks? In a bagel factory?" you hear him rail against the mechanic.

The truck comes alive again. "About time," shouts the bearded elf. He guns the motor and speeds past the barrier. Your eyes follow his trail of dust for a few seconds and then he disappears beyond a sand dune.

Somewhere along the line someone opens up with automatic fire. You can't tell from which side. You wonder about Ivan.

The Road to Terror

You meet Ronnie at an air base in Sinai a short time after his return from a combat mission. You had known this six-footer with the gentle voice and hazel eyes in civilian life, and so the conversation over coffee comes easy.

"At the beginning, it was all *kef*, pure pleasure, but then things happen to you. Perhaps it's a matter of getting a bit older. I'm thirty now and I've been flying for about ten years. My reactions and frame of reference aren't the same any longer. War is no longer merely a dangerous competition. You wake up one morning and you understand that war really means killing and that as a consequence people die. You don't want to be one of those people because by the time you're my age, you have some very heavy commitments.

"No, I don't believe that I'm ever really frightened while flying. You build up a tremendous confidence after a while—in the aircraft itself, in the maintenance, in your own ability to cope with almost any situation. You know you'll never be left stranded by your buddies. After all, everything is a matter of percentages, even crossing Dizengoff Street at four in the afternoon, and you know that the odds are with you. But with accumulated experience, there are certain events which stand

115

out. They impress themselves on your brain and you're never the same man again.

"During the Six Day War I was a squadron leader. One of our ground units fighting on the West Bank ran into some stiff enemy resistance, and air support was requested. When we arrived, there was heavy ground fire from some armored vehicles but we were already flushed with victory. According to the books, it should have gone easily. On the second run, I heard the voice of my wingman on the radio. He was trying to speak into the microphone but instead of words I just heard sounds that seemed to be floating in water. There was something terrible about his inability to communicate. I felt that he was trying to reach out and say something to me but there was a curtain of air between us. We had served for many years together. For the first time in my life, I felt completely helpless.

"I stared out of the canopy and saw a thin finger of smoke rising around his cockpit. Then the plane just seemed to collapse. It reminded me of a bird whose wings have been broken. It nosed into the ground and there was a stunning explosion. It looked as if the whole landscape had been eaten away by a wave of napalm.

"I guess we all went a little crazy then. I admit that it was unreasonable; after all, we were trying to kill them and they were trying to kill us. We fired everything we had. We returned to base without a single spare bullet in the entire squadron.

"I tried to analyze my feelings then, but I couldn't. I still can't. I know that I felt hatred, but it wasn't the hatred of seeing a friend killed. We're taught to expect things like that in war. It had something to do with the

116

unspoken terror with which he died. He was trying to reach out and communicate, and there was nothing that anyone in the world could do for him. Those unspoken words still haunt me. I guess they always will.

"I'm a psychology buff, and for a long time now I've been trying to figure out what I feel toward the enemy. I know it's good fashion to say that we don't hate, but that's a lot of crap. We're learning to hate, but it's a kind of hatred born of frustration. It's a feeling you develop because you see no end to the conflict and you're nearly dead certain that this is the kind of legacy you'll be passing on to your children. It's an emotion bred of tension. The enemy says Egypt can afford to lose twenty battles but Israel can lose only one. You hate him because he's so right and because he has put his finger on the nerve of your vulnerability.

"But there's something even more frightening. I've tried to analyze my feelings when I'm on a bomb run. There are a lot of conflicting emotions, but one thing stands out—power. I know that my index finger contains the power of life and death. I know I can swoop down and destroy a hundred lives in seconds. I know I'm driving 25,000 pounds of airplane and that I'm generating thousands of pounds of thrust. I see a mushroom of smoke and I feel a tingle of strength. The earth is too far away to think of fellow human beings. I've become a sort of demigod."

Ronnie pauses and then smiles bitterly.

"And I'll tell you something. I hate myself for the revelation. I'm sick of blood and tired of my own vicarious thrills. I don't want the life of another human being on my conscience. But you see, what I want or don't want really doesn't matter, and the proof is that I'll be over Egypt again before too long."

Ronnie is silent. You can't think of a thing to say. You are thinking that war provides people with some unusual insights into their own character and frailties. And not only the men on the line, but the people involved in this war through their relationships with these men.

You remember Haim, a twenty-year-old farmer's son who always complained that he was born with two left feet and ten thumbs. The only sensible thing he ever did in his life was to fall in love with Leah, only eighteen and lovely. Haim stepped on a mine one quiet Saturday morning, and his two left feet and six of his ten thumbs were blown across the uneven floor of the desert.

After months of hovering between life and death, Haim called off his engagement to Leah. He said he would not burden his fiancée with a hopeless cripple. To himself he contemplated suicide.

Leah had her own views, however. She insisted on going through with the marriage. She said that she loved him—the man, the person. The shells continued to fall in Sinai, and Leah and Haim were married.

This was once a railroad station on a branch line stretching eastward from Kantara. It has long since been dismantled but there are still a couple of lonely, shabby buildings rising out of the sand dunes of northern Sinai to attest to this earlier link with Egypt. Today, it is the site of an Israeli army camp, a solitary outpost composed of tents, bunkers and igloo-type buildings; of girl soldiers dressed in colorful bell-bottom slacks; of tired, dirty troops returning from patrols; of a wide, remarkably clean mess hall; of a small, makeshift hospital; of a synagogue; and of the treaded and wheeled vehicles of war.

It is the eve of the Sabbath, and by eight o'clock the mess hall has filled with scrubbed troops, the girl soldiers wearing their Sinai finery—everything from form-fit slacks to wondrous miniskirts. The long tables are covered with food and bottles of Sabbath wine, and everyone is obsessed by the thought of food. The forks remain untouched, however, because the Sergeant for Religious Affairs (a uniquely Israeli rank) has not yet intoned the Kiddush—the benediction over the Sabbath wine. There is a certain amount of hungry grumbling, and the flaxen-haired lieutenant sitting next to you suggests ganging up on the sergeant when he arrives.

121

After a few minutes the sergeant appears and begins reciting the ancient liturgy. Midway through, there is the rasping shriek of the air-raid siren, and the cup of wine he holds is elbowed into his chest as the soldiers rush out of the mess hall toward the bunkers.

"The bastard sergeant," a faceless, breathless voice exclaims as we wait in darkness. "I didn't even have a piece of bread."

"The soup will be cold," a girl laments, the desert cold creeping under her miniskirt.

"Someday Egypt and I are going to have it out personally," a young voice grumbles. "Trying to blow us up is one thing, but trying to starve us is downright inhuman."

The all-clear sounds and as you make your way back to the mess hall, you look up at the sky full of stars. Was it a Mig or a Sukhoi, you wonder, and for a moment you imagine the young pilot of the unidentified plane, up there alone in the darkness. You feel frightened. You return to your cold soup and a table stained by spilt wine.

Later in the evening, you meet the Sergeant for Religious Affairs. Tall, heavily bearded, twenty-one years old and a former citizen of Morocco, Menachem laments his fate.

"Who asked for this job? Not me! Is it my fault that I studied in a religious high school for three years? This is the worst job in the army. Everyone thinks I'm queer. What's so strange about being religious? Someone has to do it.

"I told them that I'm not even authentic. I became religious only a few years ago. Up to this very day, I can't even eat in my own parent's home. The food isn't kosher enough. I could have stood on my head and it wouldn't have helped. In this army nobody asks you what you want to do. They notice that you studied religion for a while and then the sadists victimize you. Sure, I could have refused, but God knows what they would have done to me.

"The troubles I've had. About eight months ago I stopped an officer from taking out a half-track on Friday night. I told him that if it wasn't operationally urgent, he would be breaking the *halachah*. What's so strange about that? I was merely performing my duty. I know of a case where an officer for religious affairs made a general walk a mile because he wouldn't allow him to drive his jeep into the compound on the Sabbath. And the officer was only a second lieutenant. Think of it!

"So this officer began cursing me. He said that I was holding up the war. I got angry and told him, war or no war, no nonessential driving on Friday night. Then you know what he did? He noticed that my shirt pocket was unbottoned. He had me restricted to base for thirty days. You think this is an easy job?"

Almost every Israeli unit has either a noncom or officer in charge of religious affairs. Their primary duties are to make certain that *kashruth* is observed and that the Sabbath laws are not violated except when absolutely essential. They attend to the religious needs of the men and, when they die, to their bodies before burial.

"I'm only twenty-one, but I've already seen so much death I want to vomit," says Menachem. "You see your friends go out on patrol in the morning and then someone brings back their bodies in the afternoon. Have you ever seen a man after a shell finishes with him? They bring me

123

pieces. Sometimes I want to tear the hair out of my head. I'll tell you the truth, I need a holiday. This desert and this rotten war are making my soul stink. When I get out, I'm going to become a hermit."

You leave Menachem and retire to your bunker to get some sleep. But you wake early, waiting for the patrol to set off which will take you to the war-torn city of Kantara and then further north to one of the distant outposts wedged in the teeth of the enemy. This is the only area where Egypt retains a foothold on the Sinai peninsula.

During the Six Day War Israeli armor broke through Egyptian positions in the Gaza Strip and fanned out throughout Sinai, in lightning strokes, to wrest the area from Nasser's army by obtaining control of the three major arteries cutting across the desert and wilderness. From Sharm-el-Sheikh in the south to Kantara in the north, Egyptian positions crumbled one after the other. But because of a unique set of geographical circumstances in the far north, where much of the land is a giant bog unsuitable for the movement of armor, Egyptian forces were able to retain control of a tiny splinter of Sinai until the cease-fire was called into effect on June 11.

This solitary Egyptian enclave on the east bank of the Canal, with its string of heavily reinforced fortresses stretching down from Port Fuad, poses a serious tactical problem for Israel. It is no accident that Israeli casualties are highest in the northern sector of the front.

The problem in the north is essentially one of topography. Much of the land on both sides of the Canal is composed of light sand which is moistened and loosened by seeping underground water, making vehicular traffic

124

impossible. Even large-scale movements of foot troops are difficult on the sand basin. The lake waters feeding in from a huge Mediterranean lagoon have created a tactical nightmare for the operations people. A giant bowl of near quicksand isolates the Israelis' northernmost positions, and the only access to the forward citadels north of Kantara is a narrow stretch of sand no wider than twenty yards and partially exposed to Egyptian positions across the Canal.

Closer to the Mediterranean, the sand is firm and consequently adaptable to tank and other armor movements. It is also the critical area where the main coastal road leads like an arrow to El Arish, Gaza and Tel Aviv and hence an area of immense strategic importance to Israel. Since the sea borders the entire area, and recognizing the quantitative superiority of the Egyptian navy, Israeli forces must be constantly on their guard to prevent a marine landing which would enable Egyptians to deploy in Sinai and consolidate their forces for a massive breakthrough.

Yet a third problem is the Mediterranean lagoon which permits Egyptian naval forces to slip into waters east of the Canal and hammer away at the Israeli positions.

The major problem, however, is the narrow stretch of sand which is the one lifeline to the string of northern fortresses and the most perilous area in terms of Egyptian commando forays, ambushes, mines and artillery duels. To complicate the matter, every vehicle making the run spews great clouds of dust into the air so that detection from the opposite bank is almost inevitable.

You lie on your cot, your perspiring face covered with

flies, waiting for the paratrooper supply unit to pick you up.

Someone kicks your door open. "The half-track will be at the entrance to the camp in five minutes," a soldier announces. "Be ready."

Five minutes, you think. Not an awfully long time. Just enough seconds to check that your canteen is full, to test for the reassuring click of your revolver, to tighten the straps on your knapsack, to destroy a few more of the insects that seem to be devouring you alive. You adjust the strap on your helmet. It must fit snugly but not so tight that it suffocates you when you begin bobbing up and down in the armored personnel carrier. Finally, you don the flak jacket. You zip it closed and you can already feel your body fighting for ventilation. In another few seconds, there will be a river of sweat down your back. You give the cot a quick pat. It is ugly, worn and sand-embedded, but it will be good to be sleeping there again. Then you step out into the sunlight.

There are six men on the vehicle, silent and tired. They have been making this trip for what seems an eternity. They know the ugly dangers of traveling at low speeds under the sights of one of the heaviest artillery concentrations in the world. They have seen so much bloodshed in their eighteen or nineteen years that they have developed a certain fatalism. Why him and not me? Every bullet is marked, they say.

You anchor yourself to the rear of the vehicle and hang on for dear life. The first part of the trip, until you hit Kantara, is on asphalt and the driver treats the lumbering vehicle as if it were an Austin-Healy traveling down an Italian expressway. A few miles down the flat road you see your first tank. It is a Patton A-3 and the crew waves as you pass. Their sun-scorched faces are caked in grime.

The armored personnel carrier is manned by paratroopers. It is one of the anomalies of this war, conducted along static lines, that Israel has committed many of its crack offensive battalions to a defensive holding action. As usual, the average age of the men is under twenty. The major difference is that most of these men hail from *moshavim* and *kibbutzim*, and all are volunteers for the paratroop units.

Israel's paratroopers have distinguished themselves in all of its battles since the State was declared. The Sinai confrontation is no exception. It was the paratroopers who bore the heaviest brunt of the hand-to-hand fighting during the Six Day War. Again, it was they who were given the mission of lightning punitive raids against terrorist bases in Jordan and Lebanon. In 1956 it was the paratroopers who fell behind enemy lines to block the retreat at Mitla. The sands of Sinai are familiar terrain to them.

As you approach Kantara, you know that on either side, deeply concealed in the desert, are the backup forces—the mobile artillery and tanks which are Israel's steel sinew on the Canal. These are the modern Bedouin. They have no homes. The sand is their bed. They move relentlessly, never permitting the enemy to achieve a fix on their positions.

One of the sandy-haired paratroopers wordlessly hands you a menthol candy. What is there to say on a day such as this? He removes a letter from inside his flak jacket from a childhood sweetheart who grew up with him on the shores of the Sea of Galilee. He closes his eyes for a moment and tries to recollect her features, but the dust wipes away all memories.

Kantara is the only major city on the Canal that fell into Israeli hands. All the other major population centers—Port Said, Port Fuad, Kantara West, Ismailia and Suez—are on the Egyptian side of the Canal. What is left of Kantara is wretched desolation and silence. The mosque and its thin minaret still stand, but most of the mud-brick houses are crumbling. There are huge craters around the stately date palms, and the only signs of life are the birds which flutter and chirp in the bright morning sun.

During the period immediately after the war, Kantara was still a living town and there were Arab peddlers and fish restaurants. Then came the gloom of artillery, and almost all the former residents chose repatriation to Egypt. Kantara stands, but it is a ghost town.

The asphalt ends and your vehicle leaps from the road to a cratered path. Suddenly the world becomes a film of swirling orange particles as the suffocating and blinding dust rises from the ground. The precariousness of your position gnaws at your guts, and it takes all your will power to remain calm.

The paratroopers are intently silent. They have churned this same sand endless times and they have seen the dunes sweep over the bodies of their fallen comrades. Someone tries to light a cigarette, but the turbulent air makes it impossible. Somewhere in front is the dust of another vehicle. You begin to speculate. Will the Egyptian gunners concentrate their fire on the lead vehicle or will it arouse their attention to the whole line of movement

so that they'll turn their battery of guns in your direction? You are startled by your thoughts. It is as if you are willing to sacrifice the boys on the first vehicle so that you can remain alive to see another sunset.

The vehicle stops abruptly. Since there must be a safe distance between transports, your armored personnel carrier is ordered to halt. Waiting under the broiling sun, you feel the grit of sand between your teeth. Accidentally you touch the barrel of a machine gun and the hot metal blisters your hand. Somehow the pain feels good. It reminds you that there is a reality. Meanwhile the driver jumps down, nonchalantly unbuttons his pants and urinates his initials on the sand.

"You're getting good, Haim," someone tells him.

"That's nothing," answers the driver as he buttons up. "If you were a good-looking girl instead of a dog face, I would really show you something."

"Talk, talk," another soldier says. "It is a well-known fact, Haim, that you are a notorious eunuch."

"Better a eunuch than a fairy like you," replies Haim.

"It takes one to know one," comes the retort.

"Nu, why the delay today?" asks one of the soldiers as he removes his goggles and lights a cigarette.

"Too many tourist buses," answers Haim. "All the Scandinavian broads are upsetting the traffic pattern."

"You know what I'm going to do when I get out of this miserable army?" queries the sandy-haired soldier. "I'm going to write a tourist guide to Suez. I'll have it published in English, Hebrew and Arabic and make a fortune. What could be nicer than this? Blue waters to bathe in, plenty of healthy sunshine, a little bit of fishing."

"And flies," someone interrupts.

"What's wrong with flies so long as they're kosher? I've seen a few very religious boys swallow them."

You ask the men about their commander. You have heard a lot about him.

"He's a prince. They don't make men like that any more. He's one of the really great fighters in the army, and what's more, he's so religious that he won't even tie his shoelaces on the Sabbath."

"Do you know that when one of his men gets killed, he cries. I'm not joking. I saw it myself. He cried like a baby, God bless him."

"You may not know it but he's also a scholar. He has a master's degree from the university. I'm not sure what he studied, but I think it was humanities."

You are reminded of Orde Wingate, the British mystic-soldier who taught Jews military tactics in the late thirties because he believed in the destiny of the Jewish people and their right to return to their ancient homeland.

"Maybe he's a scholar and maybe he's orthodox, but most important of all he's a fighter. There's practically no part of his body that hasn't been carved up by Arab bullets. He was so badly shot up during the Six Day War that it's a miracle he's alive today, much less that he's still commanding a paratrooper unit."

"You're all wrong," pipes up Haim as he returns to the driver's seat. "Most important of all, he's a *mensch*, a human being. That's why we all love him."

Strange, you think, this almost spiritual rapport between Israeli officers and their men. Perhaps this is the key to the overall efficiency and morale of Zahal. There is almost total informality between the men in a classless army. They eat the same food, share the same burdens, dream the same dreams. They call each other by their first names. In action the unwritten law is that the officer goes in first, and this accounts for the staggering number of casualties among line officers. In the Israel Defense Forces the officers and enlisted men have established a camaraderie that other armies of the world find hard to believe.

The order to proceed is received, and the half-track begins cutting through the sand. The path is agonizing, but it is good to be moving again. Movement means life. It connotes a destination. It means that the day may somehow end.

You turn a bend and you see the Israeli flag. It looks so lovely and beautiful fluttering under the eyes of Egypt. It represents the site of the first fortress on the line north of Kantara, but your destination is deeper along the trail. You pass the fort in a haze of dust and continue in the direction of the mouth of the Canal.

There is the sound of an explosion, the first real reminder of war you've heard this morning. Then there is a puff of black, billowing smoke on the other side of the Canal.

"The Air Force!" someone exclaims. "Our boys are on the job again!"

The presence of the Israeli Air Force in the skies above gives you a new dimension of security. It is a simple fact of military life that men under air attack will be concentrating on other things than merely eliminating you. You hear the answering antiaircraft fire and then there is another thud and a great geyser of smoke rises from the west bank of the Canal. The men in your carrier tighten their grips on their weapons and the driver presses hard on the gas. You are three-quarters of the way there. It is all a matter of luck and fate, but for the first time this day you are reasonably convinced that you will arrive at your destination.

Minutes later you reach the outpost. "Out!" orders a corporal. "Quickly, assemble your gear and get into one of the bunkers."

It is no idle command. The enemy knows from your dust trail that you have arrived and that you are exposed. If there is any moment when he can clobber you with reasonable certainty of success, it is now. You swing from the APC and land with a thump on the sand. Your helmet strap tears at your chin as you race toward the protection of the bunkers.

"Food first," suggests Haim, and you both detour toward the mess hall. You reach for a plastic plate full of hot potatoes and meat just as someone shouts: "An incoming!" The food splatters to the ground and you and Haim race toward the nearest bunker. God, you wonder, will you ever again eat a full meal in peace?

Outside, there is the sharp retort of an 82-mm. shell as it explodes about twenty yards away. You are suddenly no longer hungry.

Seated inside the bunker are five men eating dried sunflower seeds. One of them, twenty-one-year-old Uri, is the commander of the outpost. He is of medium height and has dark wavy hair and a good strong chin. He looks pathetically young for such responsibility, but if you've learned nothing else you know that war here is the game of youth.

"Have some seeds," he suggests as a second shell

falls near the fort. You remove your helmet and flak jacket and feel a sluice of perspiration opening down your back.

"How's the outside world?" asks Yitzhak, a sergeant from a border settlement in the north who sported a red handlebar mustache.

"It goes on," you reply as you wipe your face with a dirty rag of a handkerchief.

"Welcome to the Suez Hilton," says nineteen-year-old Bennie from Tel Aviv. "Our linen is a little soiled and room service is not on a par with Tel Aviv, but our sunflower seeds are the best in Sinai and we provide our guests with fireworks displays almost every day, the Sabbath included."

"How do you, as paratroopers, feel being confined in a citadel instead of doing the work you were trained for?" you ask at the first moment's quiet.

"We do what we're told to do," Uri answers. "At the beginning it was hard. It's difficult to be confined in such a small area and to be under constant threat of enemy shells. We're taught to be the initiators of action. Now we find ourselves on the receiving end all the time. But someone has to do this work and I imagine there is nothing more important today to the State of Israel than holding these forts. Frankly, I'll be just as happy when Sinai is behind me, but in the meantime we do what we can."

"The hard part," says Yitzhak, staring you full in the face with a pair of serious eyes, "is when you lose your friends. The boys who were ambushed and butchered recently were friends with whom we had gone through training. When we heard about their deaths, we were all in a state of shock for a few hours. You get used to hearing about casualties, but to have so many of your comrades die so suddenly is something else. It's not a matter of fear. I don't even think it's a matter of anger. People are supposed to die in wars. Mostly it's sadness and frustration. They were all so damn young. I guess half of them had never even known a woman."

"We are the dying virgins," says Bennie. "We are untainted. We go right to Paradise."

"You know," says Uri, "I wish there was a way of taking everybody in Israel on a armored-car tour of the line. We know that they are worried about us and we hear stories of panic because of the Russians. I would like them to see how high the morale is here. I would like them to see for themselves the comradeship that exists on this side of the Canal.

"I've seen crazy things since I've been here. I saw a man disobey my orders and race outside into an artillery barrage because he thought one of his friends hadn't heard the announcement of an incoming shell. I punished him afterwards, but I loved him more than ever. Don't ever tell him what I said though. He still thinks I'm a jackass."

"This is a nutty war," says Yitzhak, "because people still aren't convinced that it's war. The Egyptians are much clearer on the issues than we are. How many times does someone have to tell you that he's going to kill you before you finally believe him?"

"Itzsy, you talk too much," says Bennie. "You're a good fighter, but you exercise your mouth too much. Have some seeds and shut up. Uri, tell him what you did on the fifth of June."

Uri shakes his head negatively.

"Tell him," insists Bennie.

"You notice," says Uri, "that we have a flagpole here but no flag? It's because of orders. There's a lot of wind here and our people were afraid that the flapping would attract enemy aircraft. Well, on the fifth of June, I felt miserable. First of all, it was my birthday. Secondly, it was three years since the Six Day War, so I decided to do something which I had never done before. I disobeyed a direct order. We hoisted the Star of David right over the heads of the entire Egyptian army. When it began waving in the wind, one of the boys cried. It was like a holiday in the fort. Even the food tasted better. I kept the flag flying for three days. It's our flag. I didn't give a damn if it attracted not only the Egyptian Air Forces but the whole Soviet Union. Those three days were some of the happiest in my life."

Hard work, fatigue, the steady grind of tension seem not to affect the high morale of the troops on the firing line.

"It's because we can get home," explains Yitzhak. "That's the secret. We know that under normal circumstances, we can get back to our families for a couple of days every month or so. I don't care how long I have to travel. When I see my mother, everything is OK. We can also telephone home on occasion. You don't know what it means. You tell your mother you're fine and she cries and you tell her to stop crying and all the time you feel like crying yourself. You know, we Jews are a bunch of criers. It's a wonder we can win any war."

Another shell explodes outside. Not long ago, the Egyptians fired 3,000 shells in the course of three hours on this fort.

There must have been men like these, you think, in the time of Masada, in the era of the Maccabees, during the War of Independence. As you stare into the faces of these young paratroopers, you know why Israel will not lose the battle of Sinai. You hope that your daughters will one day bring home men of this caliber.

The sun is beginning to sink. Someone taps you on the shoulder and informs you that an APC will be passing in a few minutes. You step outside. The flagpole is standing naked and erect and you can almost see the flag.

Artillery and Tanks

After trudging for almost a mile, you climb up a pyramid of light orange sand and stare out into the distance. You spot the camouflaged artillery unit—your destination—about a quarter of a mile ahead. Knowing that your trek in the wilderness is almost at an end, you collapse in a bed of soft sand for a few minutes to drink in the incredibly beautiful and desolate scenery that surrounds you.

Directly west you can see two distinct lines of date palms—one representing the Israeli border, the other Egypt. You hear the dull, thudding rumble of war as Israeli airplanes burst out of the clouds and blast Egyptian positions in the north. You discern tiny flashes of light in the azure sky as the wings of the aircraft catch the sunlight.

Only 100 yards away to the south, palm fronds wave in the warm, dry desert air. It is another one of those tiny islands of green which dot Sinai and somehow serve to highlight the loneliness and desolation of the landscape.

As you lift your canteen to your sun-cracked lips, you notice a few small, sparrowlike birds sand-bathing at the fringe of the oasis. It strikes you as remarkable that life can exist under these difficult conditions and that there is a type of bird life indigenous to Sinai. Somehow, many years ago, they made their peace with nature, existing on the flies, bees and other insects that flourish in the oases. In addition to the sparrowlike creatures, the skies of Sinai are shared by the Israel Air Force and birds of prey. The desert is home to eagles and vultures, the latter preying on carrion and garbage, the former subsisting on small animals and other birds. Sinai is also an important way station for the huge clouds of storks moving from Europe to Africa in the fall and then back in the spring.

In your travels through the desert, you had seen no wildlife but there had been spoors. Amiram, your friend and guide in the Central Mountains, had pointed to these as evidence of the presence of foxes, hyenas, rabbits, gazelles, wild goats, porcupines and even wolves and coyotes.

Now in your sand bed watching the birds, your thoughts return to an earlier incident of the day. On the way down to the artillery post, you had come across an Israel Army truck, apparently abandoned in the wasteland.

Although sizzling in the midday heat, the truck appeared intact. You and your companions had cocked your guns as you descended from the jeep and fanned out in opposite directions. The silence was eerie. Suddenly a voice called out, "Shalom! Shalom!" The shock of the human utterance was so intense that only a miracle can explain the fact that no one opened fire as a purely automatic response.

A medium-sized and darkly good-looking soldier emerged from behind a nearby sand dune, grinning at us with a set of perfect ivory teeth. His Uzzi was dangling carelessly from his shoulder.

"What the hell is going on here?" one of the men

asked in a no-nonsense tone.

"Can't you see? The truck broke down," the soldier replied. "I think it's the carburetor."

"How long have you been here?"

"I don't know," shrugged the soldier. "I guess about thirty hours."

You and your companions exchanged glances.

"I have some water," anticipated the soldier. "And a truck passed earlier and left me some cheese and waffles."

"Did you try to fix the truck?"

"I'm a driver, not a mechanic."

"Why didn't you go back for help?"

"Who would watch the truck?"

"But what have you been doing all this time?"

"I've been sitting."

"Been thinking of anything particular?"

He shrugged. "I told you. I was just sitting."

"Well, then come back with us. We'll get a mechanic to go back with you."

"No," he said. "Someone will come sooner or later. I'll just sit here until he arrives."

After a long time in the desert, something seems to click off in the human brain. A certain apathy infiltrates the body. The rhythm of the sand mesmerizes. It is a dangerous phenomenon, more dangerous than the forces of Cairo. You have seen this in Africa as well. After traveling forty miles into the veldt, you had discovered a single Masai warrior leaning on his spear, staring out across the verdant plain without moving a muscle, a human rock in the wilderness.

You rouse yourself from your recollections, scramble

down the dune and head in the direction of the artillery camp. On the outskirts are three empty beer bottles, a soap wrapper and a towel hanging out to dry on a desert bush.

In many ways the life of the artillery men is even more difficult than that of the troops manning the fortifications. It is true that their mobility provides a measure of safety, but they have no cots, no mess halls, no electricity, no permanent quarters. They are desert nomads in the fullest sense of the words.

Their security, of course, depends on motion. The Egyptians have been provided with the latest devices to monitor shots fired from the Israeli side. Israel knows that she cannot match Egypt with firepower. The Egyptian artillery concentration along Sinai includes, among others, 150 self-propelled guns, 600 truck-mounted rocket launchers and 35 tactical missile batteries. Israel's only chance is lightning response and then immediate evacuation.

If there is any branch of the military in which the Egyptians can distinguish themselves, it is artillery. Ever since World War II, the Soviet Union has been the world's strongest advocate of concentrated artillery barrages, and this was the first of their tactical legacies to Cairo.

Unlike the Israelis, who depend on mobility, the Egyptians have set their batteries in fixed sites which only a direct hit can damage or destroy. This is why so much of the burden of retaliating against Egyptian shellings has fallen on the Israel Air Force.

Israel's answer to the Egyptian artillery threat has been ingenuity. By cutting away the turret of Super-Sherman tanks and mounting 155-mm. guns, thus creating

144

a mobile artillery platform, Israel has succeeded in compensating to some degree for its relative paucity of equipment.

"We are Bedouins," explains twenty-one-year-old Lieutenant Amos, son of a Tel Aviv greengrocer. "We must be constantly on the alert. We sleep when we can—and near our artillery pieces—because we never know when we'll receive orders to open fire. There's also the threat of air attack. The Egyptian Air Force has tried to locate us a few times. So far, touch wood, they haven't succeeded.

"We don't try to fool ourselves by saying that life is easy. It's damned hard living out here in the desert. You don't only miss your comforts, you miss your family and friends. That's why we try to send the men home on leave for about a week every month. Otherwise we would all go crazy.

"What do I do when I get home? Well, the first thing is a shower. We have plenty of water here and I guess there is even enough for everyone to shower a couple of times a week, but it's not the same. Here you wash up and a few minutes later you're sticky again. If it's not the sand, it's the sweat. You can never really be clean in the desert. Everytime you move, you perspire. You drink gallons of water and it just seeps out of every pore.

"Well, after the shower, I have a wonderful meal—not just regular good food but the special things my mother knows I like. I'm not complaining about army food, but they don't cook just for me the way my mother does. We have our own kitchen here and more than enough food. I think the army's food is getting better all the time. We have plenty of fresh fruit and vegetables.

Most of the other food is canned, and the final product really depends on the cook.

"After I'm fed, I visit my girl. Well, I don't really have one girl, I have a few, but I think I like one of them better than the rest.

"Finally, I sleep. We never get enough sleep here. You see, we sleep because we're exhausted. There's no pleasure in that kind of sleep. Part of the brain is always awake. You keep expecting orders even when you doze off. When I get back home, I sleep. At the beginning, my mother used to wake me up because she thought I was dead. I guess I must have slept for about fifteen hours once and never even moved."

You notice a pool of blue water out in the distance and ask Amos about it.

He laughs. "It's a mirage. Everyone asks us about that 'lake'. You would have a pretty dry swim there."

Gabi is just over eighteen. His parents live in Beer-sheva, and he is one of thirteen children. "We're very religious Syrian Jews," he explains modestly. Gabi has his own ideas on how the war should be run. He hands you a warm bottle of Coca Cola as he elaborates.

"Jews are too soft-hearted. I was only a little boy when my parents brought me here from Damascus, but I can tell you that if we treated the Arabs half as badly as they treated the Jews, they would have learned their lesson by now.

"After the Six Day War, instead of acting like victors we behaved as though we were ashamed of winning. Instead of concentrating on our own security, we began working for Arab welfare. Well, if you think they appreciate what we did for them, you are a fool. Today you

take your life in your hands if you go shopping in Gaza.

"God Almighty, do you have any idea what they would have done to Tel Aviv and Jerusalem if they had won? Do you know how the Syrians treat our prisoners? I'd give them a taste of their own medicine. That's the only language they understand. That's what they have been taught to understand."

The conversation depresses you, and you are grateful when the Shekem truck pulls to a grinding halt in a cloud of sand. Shekem, the Israeli version of the American PX chain, supplies nonmilitary items to the troops and represents a chapter of unsung heroism in the Sinai theater of war. Wherever there are soldiers, no matter how isolated the citadel or precarious the route, the civilian drivers of Shekem arrive on a routine basis. In order to transport their cargo of chocolate bars, cold soft drinks, chewing gum and cigarettes, they may pass through a barrage of shells, machine gun fire or snipers' bullets. Shekem trucks have been riddled by enemy fire, drivers have been wounded and kidnapped, and yet the "sweets lift" continues. An iced drink may seem like a small facet of a serious war, but to the troops buried under sand it takes on a special significance.

The same is true of the mail, often delivered under terrifying conditions. These are the small comforts and reminders of the outside world which keep an army fighting.

You enter into a serious argument with Amos. As your host, he insists on paying for the cokes. Knowing that he earns about ten dollars a month, you have the money ready, but Amos pulls his rank and you quench your thirst at his expense.

"The secret of maintaining morale here is rather simple," he says as you munch a vanilla-flavored waffle. "Fortunately, this is not like Vietnam. No one has to convince us that we should be here. For most of us, it would be inconceivable to be anywhere else. We hate the conditions. We hate the war. But the only alternative to being here is to lie down and die. Our parents have done their share, and now it's up to us.

"We try to keep personal problems under control before they blow up. I'll give you just one example. I knew that the mother of one of the men was about to undergo a very serious operation. He didn't ask to be sent home because he realized how short-handed we are. But I knew he was eating his heart out and that his mind was not here. A situation like that is not only unhealthy, it could be dangerous. So as not to embarrass him, I did a very simple thing. I arranged for him to get an early leave which had nothing to do with his mother's condition. When he came back, he was a new man and there were no guilt feelings."

"Amos, if you and your men could have one wish materialize right now in the desert, what do you think it would be?"

"Peace," answers Amos.

It takes a while for transport to arrive, and the sun is already descending before you locate a jeep to take you to your destination—a tank unit working hard in the last hours of daylight before the desert evening rolls over the land, and the armor moves to new, predetermined positions closer to the Canal.

Not since the North African campaign had the world witnessed anything on the scale of the tank battles between Egypt and Israel in 1967. Sinai with its broad, sandy expanses is a natural arena for tanks and, despite all the auxiliary assistance to be obtained from the air, the decisive conflicts are fought with armor. This was the message of the 1956 Sinai campaign. This was reiterated during the Six Day War. This will be the credo of the next conflict. The tools of Sinai are tracks and wheels. It could not be otherwise.

As usual, the Arabs maintain decided advantages in terms of available equipment. Although Israel uses only Patton A-3 tanks in Sinai, its 1,050 vehicles, consisting of a mixed bag of tanks purchased from different countries at varying intervals, must be spread along all its borders. On the other hand Egypt alone has 1,100 tanks, most of which are of the modern T-54 and T-55 class. Add to this number the nearly 600 frontline tanks in Syria, the 655 tanks of Iraq, most of them Russian-built, and the 335 tanks of Jordan and an accurate picture of the armor situation emerges.

Despite this, Israel preserves two strong advantages: the terrain is in Israel's hands and the tank corps consists of top professional officers and men. On the Canal, Israeli armor performs a number of vital functions. Since only a minimum of men are required to protect a defense line that consists of a series of strategically located posts, the tanks must provide the hide for covering the unprotected pockets, for patrolling and maintaining the security between the forts. Israeli forces are heavily outgunned; hence the tanks also double as mobile artillery pieces. They add enormously to the overall firing power of Zahal on the Canal. And the tanks act to keep the roadways open, minimizing Egyptian ambush attempts.

151

Thus Israeli armor, for the first time in history, is engaged in wholly defensive tasks, a strange postscript for those familiar with the history of the Israeli tank units that twice struck against Egypt.

One of the "tankists" is twenty-year-old Moshe from one of the border *kibbutzim* in the north. Israel is such an odd mixture of racial traits, complexions and physiques—ranging from dark, lithe Yemenites to blond, blue-eyed refugees of Poland and Germany—that it is virtually impossible to generalize about what the average Israeli looks like. But if there is no Israeli arch-type, there is a very pronounced *kibbutz* type emerging in the rural areas of the country. He usually is of medium height and solidly built. He has curly hair, a shade of blond or red. His clear eyes are most often blue, and his skin is coppered from years in the sun.

He has a farmer's pragmatic, unromantic view of sex. He has been reared in a closed society and so converses awkwardly in any other atmosphere. He has studied languages in school but is only at ease with Hebrew. Having been brought up communally, he is extremely self-reliant, whether he is repairing a tractor or preparing a six-course meal. Israel is the focal point of his universe. He knows every moment of her history; he indentifies most closely with the ancient Israelites and has trouble reconciling ghettoism to his concept of the Jewish people.

He is intimately acquainted with the flora and fauna, the wadis and mountains of his land and has acquired an amazing knowledge about them. He has difficulty expressing his emotions. He hates shoes, is happiest barefoot but will compromise to the extent of wearing sandals.

He gives the impression of being earthy, but he knows more about Beethoven and Gothic architecture than most of his city cousins. He will not speak about his country, but he loves it with an almost mystical passion. Serving in the frontline is as natural for him as breathing.

This is the prototype of the young *kibbutznik*, and this is Moshe.

"Life here may seem hard to you, but it really isn't. We have plenty of food, more than enough water, reading material and the army sends us some entertainers almost every week.

"Our bed is the desert, and I guess if there is one enemy besides Egypt, it's the sand. When you're driving through the desert, it chokes you. During the day, it gets so hot you can barely walk on it. In the evening, it's your mattress, and it's like sleeping on ice. I hate the sand even though sometimes it's beautiful, particularly at sunset.

"We've been lucky. We've lost only one man from our unit so far. He was our commander. He was twenty-five and came from Jerusalem. It happened on the first day that we were on the front. A sniper slammed a bullet into his head as he was peering out of the turret. That loss changed us. I'm not sure how. Remember, it was only our first day and we were all green. It's hard to analyze your feelings when someone you've lived with and trained with and eaten with is killed in front of your eyes. You feel fear and anger and mostly shock. You know that people die in war, but it's something impersonal until it strikes home. Worst of all is that it happened on the first day. You try not to think about it, but your mind tells you that if he died on the first day, then the chances of anyone surviving are limited. You know the others are thinking the same thing because they're morose and uncommunicative. It takes days before you recover.

"I've heard a lot about the fancy new Russian tanks. I don't think that any of us are too worried about them. You can tell the Russians for me that we're waiting for them. The Russians are still thinking in terms of Stalingrad. But there's an error in their judgment because we're Stalingrad now. They're the fascists threatening our country and we're the defenders. Yes, tell them we're waiting and tell them that Israel won't be a pushover."

Ya'acov has been in Israel four years and still speaks Hebrew with a strong South African accent. He lives in Haifa where his father owns a business which will some day, he supposes, be his. He is tall and freckled. He will celebrate his twentieth birthday in November.

"What I can't understand is the Americans. The Russians' activities are obvious. They want to take over the entire Middle East and then all of Africa. The only ones standing between Russia and its ambitions are the Israelis. You'd think the American State Department would appreciate this.

"Look, we're not asking for American troops. We're not even demanding free arms, although God knows the Americans could afford to be more generous with us. All we're saying is that they should supply us with the equipment we need and that they should warn the Russians against any further direct involvement. I get the feeling that there's a chess game going on between the Kremlin and Washington, with the Russians taking all the initiative.

"No, I never even think of South Africa. I don't even want to go back there on a vacation. Apartheid is

154

one of the ugliest things man has ever done. It's sort of like what the Nazis did to the Jews, only the South Africans are destroying the blacks slowly. It's funny but in South Africa, I always thought about color. You couldn't help thinking about it. The government wouldn't let you forget. Here, in Israel, the opposite is true. I've become completely color blind. My best friend is an Iraqi and he's so dark I could never get him into a hotel in Durban. My girl friend is a Yemenite. I think they're the most beautiful of all the Jews in Israel.

"What do we do in our spare time? That's a funny question. I never thought of it before. Actually, we don't have any spare time, so there's no problem. We have to keep our equipment in top condition all the time, so when we're not actually on patrol, we're taking care of the tanks. It would be hard for me to describe how many things you have to do to service a tank properly. We're kept busy most of the day and night. If we have a few spare hours, we sleep.

"I used to be a sort of insomniac. You know, I would toss around for hours before actually falling asleep. Here I once fell asleep standing up. I was leaning against a palm tree, thinking about my girl friend who had just written me a letter and the next thing I knew, I was slipping to the ground sleeping.

"I've also been gaining weight out here. I guess the fresh air is good for my appetite. When I went into the army, I weighed 130 pounds. Now I weigh 158. My mother's delighted. She always thought I was too skinny.

"No, my parents don't know where I am. Why should I worry them? They know I'm in Sinai and that's enough."

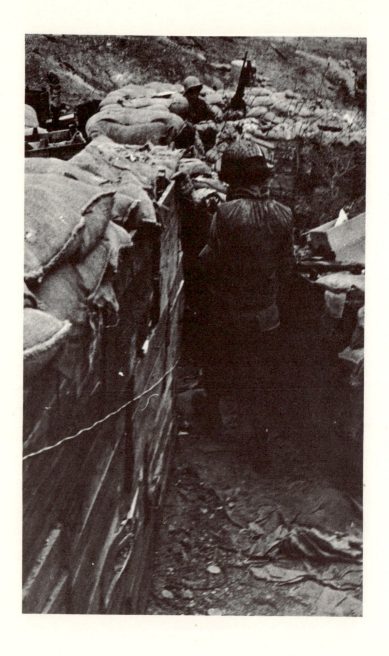

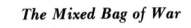

The Mixed Bag of War

On more tranquil occasions, the Chief Education Officer for Sinai, Colonel Shai, swims at the same hotel pool in Herzliya that your family uses. Today, however, when you meet there is neither place nor opportunity for swimming, and instead of a cool drink at poolside, the Egyptians are providing canapés of their own design. The enemy appears to be having a field day as the 82-mm. and 60-mm. mortar shells penetrate the confines of the fort overlooking the central sector with uncanny accuracy. The impact of the explosions is felt down in the bunker where the men are assembled. You feel safe in your cocoon of steel and sand; you think of the men above in observation posts and combat positions exposed to enemy fire.

"Shaike," as he is affectionately called by his men, is seated on an empty ammunitions crate, appraising the current military situation for the troops. He appears younger than his thirty-five years, and you suspect that the thin line of hair above his upper lip is a device to make him look older. Even so, the tall, lanky father of two, a former combat officer with the Golani Brigade, looks like a university freshman. While the shells are detonating at an average of thirty an hour, Shaike tells the troops that Zahal is on the Canal for good—or at least until an acceptable political settlement is achieved.

"I don't say that we will be here for another year or two or three. I merely say that we can remain in these positions for another hundred years if the circumstances dictate. The Egyptians have tried every tactic they could employ and, after three years, we are still here."

Indeed, you think, the Egyptians and their advisers from Odessa and Vladivostock have, since 1969, run the gamut of tactics designed to force an Israeli withdrawal from the fixed line.

During the initial stages, the citadels were blanketed by heavy artillery and mortar fire, often at point-blank range. Shells fell at the rate of thousands a week from Suez in the south to Kantara in the north, and there were comparatively heavy casualties. But after the forts had been sufficiently reinforced, the bunkers proved impervious to enemy ground fire. Even direct hits with large caliber guns have failed to seriously impair the fortifications.

In July 1969 the desperate Egyptian military leaders decided to undermine Israeli positions along the Canal by launching a series of commando attacks to penetrate and destroy the fortresses themselves. Their single success was against a tank unit damaged in a surprise attack, but no fort was ever conquered. Although eight separate attempts were made, they were all beaten back. In six instances, the corpses of commandos left behind on the Israeli side were grim evidence of the Egyptians' failure.

Later, in February 1970 Egypt decided to commit its airpower against the defense line. Supersonic Mig 21s and Sukhoi 7s swooped in low over the Canal and discharged their loads in a matter of seconds. The Egyptian

Air Force attempted to wreck the fortifications with heavy bomb stores. In the first two weeks of February, there were twenty-three separate air attacks against the citadels. During the next two weeks, the number of air forays was reduced to thirteen, and during the first two weeks of March, Egyptian air strikes dropped to three. During a single day, however, at the end of April, Egypt flew twenty-two sorties against the line and attacked a few citadels. One accurate bomb accounted for the deaths of four Israelis. On that same day, three Egyptian planes were destroyed.

During the entire Egyptian air campaign against the line, no fort was significantly damaged and only one other soldier was killed. Since then the Egyptian air offensive has petered out due to two vital factors: the increasing accuracy of Israeli antiaircraft gunners and the intensified patrolling of the Israel Air Force.

The last and final phase of Egyptian efforts to undermine the viability of the line occurred in the spring of 1970 when Egypt began a series of commando raids between the forts. Infiltrating during the evening, Egyptian units penetrated the east bank of the Canal with three objectives in mind—to plant mines, to ambush Israeli patrols and vehicles and to disrupt communications along the exposed supply routes. On one weekend, two separate Israeli patrols were ambushed and there were heavy losses. Since then Zahal has stepped up its vigorous patrolling of the "unprotected areas" between the forts and its observation of the entire terrain.

Sitting with the troops in the bunker, Shaike reviews and analyzes the military development along the Canal since the Six Day War. In short, he concludes that Israel

161

has paid a price in men and equipment but the Egyptian objective has been foiled.

"I am as honest and frank as I can be with the troops," he tells you after the lecture. "We can't expect our men to preserve equanimity and morale in the face of constant danger and hardship without understanding the tactical and political implications of the war and their part in it. I want them to realize that we do make mistakes, and as a consequence we do lose men, but that we learn rapidly and never permit the enemy to maintain the initiative for very long.

"You see, we are faced with two fundamental variables on the front. One is morale, which is a more or less steady factor and can be measured scientifically. The other is more ephemeral—it is the *matzav ruah*, the mood or state of mind of the men. You lose your friend in combat and your mood obviously is black, but it doesn't necessarily mean that your morale has dropped. As long as you know what you're doing and why you're doing it, your morale can remain high despite all sorts of personal setbacks and tragedies."

Shaike, who studied psychology at the university, pauses for a moment while a trooper elbows his way through the narrow bunker and succeeds in stepping on both your feet while butting Shaike in the face with his Uzzi.

"There are a number of psychological problems which are strictly indigenous to the static defense line and which we must take into consideration if we want to keep the morale—as opposed to the mood factor which we can't control—at a high level. For example, although we try to maintain a reasonable rotation pattern in the

162

fortresses, some soldiers—like the tank men—are required to spend most of their three-year tenure in Sinai. Obviously, this poses a problem.

"Another consideration is the distance from home. Remember that we are rather spoiled. Normally, a soldier serves only a few hours away from his home. In Sinai, we face a different situation; it can take a man ten or twelve hours to reach home from the frontline forts.

"Then we have to consider the specific conditions of serving in the desert. Standing in the dunes, you have the impression that there's no end to the wasteland. There's an absence of greenery, a feeling of awful isolation. This phenomenon is bound to affect the soldiers after a while.

"Our men who are located in the field of operations have to adjust to what we call Bedouin conditions. They are nomads and home is simply the nearest sand dune. They have to learn to exist in the desert and to eat their meals laced with sand. On the other hand, the men in the bunkers have to adjust to the severe confinement of the forts. Their movement is rigidly restricted. They have to think twice every time they leave the bunkers.

"There is a fatigue factor as well. The men in Sinai are called on to work long and uninterrupted hours. We can schedule recreation and sleep breaks, but it doesn't always depend on us. We have partners to the program on the other side of the Canal, so it depends on the volume and intensity of enemy activity.

"Then there are the additional difficulties of work schedules which, because of the exigencies of war, can never really be stabilized and fixed, and there are difficult assignments that are constantly thrust at the men—

such as patrols—which eventually take their toll.

"Israel is not a homogeneous country and that can sometimes create a big problem. You may find yourself with a tightly confined group of men who are from a dozen different backgrounds—some of them unsure of themselves in Hebrew, others recently arrived from overseas—and you have to create a compact, fighting unit out of them. It isn't easy, but it's one of the major psychological undertakings of Zahal.

"Two other points we have to consider are that we're fighting a very real hot war, and that the defensive action continues. There's nothing spurious about this war. We've already been at it for quite some time."

The Israeli army has applied itself to the human problems of serving in Sinai in a number of distinctive ways. Shaike's lectures and explanations of the overall military situation are one method. Frequent rotation of personnel wherever possible is another. Perhaps one of the main morale boosters is the telephone link from the bunkers to Israel. Additionally, Shaike's unit provides the frontline troops with 3,000 books and 2,000 periodicals, and each soldier receives at least one daily newspaper every day, often the same day the paper is printed.

Every bunker is now equipped with a radio, and each fortress has its own movie equipment. Films are changed once or twice a week. The troops in the field, the men of the artillery and tank corps, view their films in specially modified, blacked-out command cars which make their desert rounds at least once each week. No matter how intense the shelling, there is regular mail delivery, and lecturers arrive at the outposts about once in three weeks to elaborate on such diverse subjects as the archaeological significance of Sinai, and pop music.

Another vital morale builder is the appearance of top Israeli entertainers who sometimes have to squeeze through shells and tracer bullets in order to keep their appointment with the men on the front.

Where entertainment is concerned, there is no one in all of Israel with the charisma of "the Package" as she is known to Zahal. A beautiful example of Israeli womanhood who floods the outposts with folk music and highly scented perfume, Yaffa Yarkoni has sung to Israeli soldiers at the front in three wars. She epitomizes the selflessness of many Israeli entertainers who, without any form of compensation, perform for the frontline troops.

"I'm furious with them," the raven-haired, dark-eyed Yaffa had confided in Tel Aviv the day before you were scheduled to leave for Sinai. "They won't let me near the bunkers anymore. They tell me it's too dangerous. I tell them that it's no more dangerous for me than for the boys in the forts. They won't listen. Did you ever try to argue with a bunch of generals?"

Yaffa's face seems to have been lifted from an old Roman coin. She has sharp clear features and a body that could be the envy of any teenager. She has three daughters. The eldest, Orit, a recently discharged noncom in the Israeli army, is a carbon copy of her internationally acclaimed mother.

"Anyway, I still get down to the rear positions at the front a few times a week. Sure, it's hard because I'm singing in a nightclub at the same time and have to leave my house at six in the morning to get to the front. But it's worth it. You know, whenever I'm overseas, I feel miserable. It's so much better to be here in a crisis. And it's even better to be on the line with the boys. That's where you find Israel. That's where you learn what the whole thing is about."

Yaffa began singing in 1948 as a soldier in the Givati Brigade. "At first I thought of it as a joke. Then the troops began saying 'Bring Yaffa,'" and so I spent the two war years as an entertainer. I met my husband in the army at that time. The poor fellow, I'm almost never home. By the time the war ended, people were asking, 'Who is that girl in khaki trousers and sandals?'

"I kept singing and then in 1956 I went to America for a while to study voice and perfect my style. When the Suez fighting broke out, I rushed back to Israel and volunteered. I'm a singer second and an Israeli first. You know what I tell the customers at the nightclub? I tell them that we want quiet, not peace. We don't even know what peace is anymore. We have been at war forever. My mind is haunted by the dead boys I knew.

"Not so long ago, a soldier called me and he said, 'Yaffa, do you remember that you made a special trip to the desert to sing to only four boys?' Sure, I remembered. They told me that the boys had been out there stranded for weeks. I gave each of them an autographed photo and called their parents personally when I returned to Tel Aviv. Then the boy began crying. 'Yaffa,' he said, 'they're all dead except me.'

"So many telephone calls like that. Sometimes the parents call to tell me that their sons are dead. They know that I was with them because they find my photograph with their belongings. I cry a lot. I have only girls but I feel as though every one of those boys is my son. So many of my boys have been killed."

You asked Yaffa if she is frightened at the front.

"I'm scared all the time. I would have to be inhuman not to be. I gave a benefit performance up in Kiryat Shmona recently after a Katyusha attack. A little girl of six handed me flowers and then burst into tears and said she was frightened of the 'boom boom.' I told her that we're all afraid of the 'boom boom,' and hugged her and we both wept together.

"I call the families of the boys every time I get home. 'Is my boy eating?' the mothers want to know. 'Has he lost weight? Does he have enough water to wash?' What a people we are! They will never beat us! Tell that to the Arabs. Tell them no matter what they do to us, no matter how many of our sons they manage to kill, we will stand firm."

Yaffa looked up at the attractive girl sergeant who had come in to tell her that a jeep was waiting for them.

"Isn't she lovely?" said Yaffa, causing the sergeant to blush. "Two seconds and we're on our way."

Yaffa turned to you again, her face suddenly solemn. "On my last trip to Sinai, one of the boys embraced me and told me not to worry. He said that I should sleep peacefully because if Zahal ever gave them the word, they would screw all the Arabs—one by one or together. 'All we need is the right word,' he said."

Yaffa rose. You had seen her during many performances but you never remembered her looking more lovely than that morning.

"You know what is really thrilling for me? Sometimes a young soldier on the front turns to me and says, 'Yaffa, I'm the son of Yitzhak. You sang for him in 1948. He has never forgotten.' It's such a wonderful feeling. We're such a strange and incredible people. Sometimes my heart almost bursts because I'm so proud to be a Jew in this day and age. All we need is quiet, just a little bit of quiet. That isn't asking for a lot, is it?''

Yaffa had departed with the attractive sergeant, and you went home to pack. There was something about the way she had empathized that was contagious. It felt awfully good to be a Jew.

Strange Bedfellows in the Desert

To quote a popular cliché, "War makes strange bedfellows," and the Sinai confrontation is no exception.

The Israeli army represents a variety of human material that stirs the imagination. There are girls and boys. There are veterans over fifty who served in at least four wars—World War II, the War of Independence, the Sinai Campaign and the Six Day War. There are Sabras and there are new immigrants speaking a babble of languages which could confound the most hardened of drill sergeants. There are the children of Europe and America and the scions of the east. There are a preponderant number of Jews but there are also Druze, Circassians and Bedouins. There is a hard cadre of regular army officers and noncoms and there are the *miluimnikim*, the reservists.

Sinai is the theater where they all come together, so you are not surprised to meet your favorite waiter, from one of the poshest restaurants in Tel Aviv, collecting garbage in Sinai. He looks healthy and brown from the desert sun and confides that he is grateful to be out of the "Dizengoff rat race."

"And the work isn't so different, " he says cunningly. "There I serve garbage and here I collect it. Actually, it is easier to collect. No one complains about the flies. Also, I'm a corporal. I have status."

In the south of Sinai, you spend an evening at an army compound and come across an unusual contingent of reservists—unusual because there seem to be so many professional men among them.

Herschel is a professor of Humanities at Tel Aviv University. He wears a trim goatee which he claims protects his chin from the sun's rays and acts as a deterrent to flies. Motke, short and brown-haired, is an accountant for the Bureau of Internal Revenue. He came to Israel via Transylvania. He is deeply religious and insists that his orthodoxy does not interfere with his profession. Kalman is thin and angular. He is an actor, playwright and producer. He is working on his third marriage and claims that this latest call-up has ruined his career forever since he was about to be signed on for a "peach of a part. The only one happy," he laments, "is my second wife. She really hates my guts, the bitch!"

Eli is a chemist. He can't understand what he is doing in Sinai when the world knows that there is a critical shortage of good chemists in the army. "It goes to show how stupid and irresponsible they are," he complains. "They probably have a truck driver dishing out pills at Tel Hashomer Hospital."

Izzy is a spectacled photographer who specializes in fashions. "Oy, if I could only have one of those high-class models with me here," he sighs.

"And what would you do with her?" asks Herschel diffidently.

"What would I do with her? Why I would take her out to the sand dunes. . . ."

172

"Yes?"

"And I would make her fill sandbags. What the hell else do you think I would do? I stink so even my own mother wouldn't let me near her. This is some way for a nice Jewish boy to spend a holiday."

"Who says this is a holiday?" chirps Kalman as he digs out the dirt from under his fingernails with a fork.

"I say it is," answers Eli belligerently, "and stop using utensils for such dirty purposes. Next you'll be using a spoon to clean out your nose."

"Or your ass," adds Izzy.

"There is something unsanitary," says Motke, "about high-priced labor like us filling sandbags. Scholarly people should be used for more subtle undertakings. The guy who put me here evidently has a grudge against the Income Tax Bureau."

"I know a chef," ruminates Kalman, "who is driving a half-track at the Canal. What an awful waste of culinary skill! If he gets killed, there will be a drop in the Tel Aviv stuffed-derma market. The whole economy will be affected."

"Speaking of kishka," says Izzy, "I would like to photograph Brezhnev's kishkas. If it wasn't for him, I would be getting laid now instead of cooking in the desert. I'm not so young anymore. How many good screwing years do I have left?"

"Try fornicating with yourself," suggests Herschel, "although from the way you smell, I wouldn't recommend it."

"Speaking of smells," says Eli, "one of you guys spends the whole evening farting up the tent. War is war, but I don't want to suffocate in my sleep."

173

"You say they're farts?" intones Izzy. "I thought one of you was queer and using high-class perfume."

A corporal enters through one flap of the tent. He is short and dark and looks about fifteen.

"I need a volunteer," he announces.

"Take him," Izzy points to Motke. "He hasn't done anything all day and besides he isn't even a Jew."

"I have five children," says Motke, "and my back hurts and my liver is upset and if I have to peel any more potatoes, I'm going to throw up. It's also a Moslem fast day and I'm an Orthodox Jew."

"You!" The corporal points to Herschel who is cowering under a blanket in the corner.

"You realize," Herschel says gravely to the corporal as he rises from the floor, "that if you ever attend Tel Aviv University, I'll flunk you."

"Poor Herschel," says Izzy, "second time consecutively. These professors have no *mazel*."

Two days later, you meet another variant of the Israeli army, twenty-year-old Yehudit Stein who is secretary to one of the top officers. Born on a kibbutz near Hadera, Yehudit later moved with her parents to Eilat where her father is the municipal secretary.

"My job?" the green-eyed Yehudit asks. "I guess I do a little of everything. We're on twenty-four-hour-a-day duty here although we normally work about fifteen hours. There's the general work of collating reports from the various outpost. I guess I'm sort of part-time waitress and short-order cook as well. There's also a lot of telephoning. I simply do whatever I'm called to do. I can drive a jeep, too, by the way."

Yehudit has a gentle face, and there is nothing

flashy or noisy about the way she moves and speaks.

"I guess the war has changed me. At least that's what my parents say. Mom tells me that she doesn't recognize me any longer. She says that my face is drawn and that I'm less communicative. It's really not the work or the tension. Probably it's because I've seen too many of my friends killed. It does change you after a while.

"I was in Eilat with my parents when I heard the news over the radio that one of our patrols had been ambushed. I'd been looking forward for weeks to being home with my family, but I couldn't stand it. I came back immediately.

"You dream of returning home but there really is no peace, even with your family. I'm always so nervous there. Every time the phone rings, my heart starts palpitating. I guess I just feel that I belong here where I'm too busy to think of other things. I don't have to imagine anything. I know.

"It seems strange, doesn't it? Here I am, only twenty, and so agitated that I can't sit still. Certainly I'm frightened. Every time there's an air alert, I'm scared. At the beginning I didn't know what it meant, and then one day the walls began to cave in around the office and it became abruptly clear—they were really trying to kill me. I assume you get used to it after a while. It's like getting used to pain, isn't it? It's hard for me to explain, but when a raid is over, it's as if my life had been returned to me. The fear passes and I just feel grateful. I don't know to whom. Maybe I'm becoming religious. I just feel this tremendous wave of gratitude.

"When the bombings started, they wanted to evacuate the girls. We refused. We threatened to go on strike.

I can understand their not permitting us on the frontline but we're useful here. We serve a purpose and we free the men for other more important duties. Besides, men panic more easily than women. Don't smile. It's a physiological fact. After an air attack, the girls recover more quickly than the men. They're annoyed to hear it but it happens to be true. Fundamentally, women are tougher than men even if they're not so strong.

"I've been here eleven months but I still feel the same tension every time the boys go out. Perhaps I'm just tired. I feel so old and exhausted. Age is a state of mind as well as body.

"We girls talk a lot about the war among ourselves. After all, that's natural. It's the one thing that preoccupies us. I've tried to analyze my feelings about the Arabs. I can get exceedingly angry at them, but there's a difference between anger and hatred. They're simply idiots. Their girls must feel exactly as I do. What joy can there be from seeing their friends killed? The Russians are something else. Yes, if I have hatred in me, it's against them. They don't belong here. They're the guilty ones because they continue to push the Arabs into war.

"In the beginning, it was very hard here. Now it's almost like living in luxury. In the early days, we slept two in a bed. There were no bathrooms. The water was severely rationed. Now we have as much as can be expected of an army camp. The food is excellent—as good as at home. We have comfortable quarters. Come, I'll show you where I live."

Yehudit's room is tiny but neat. There is a pile of records, a few books and a stuffed dog on the floor. On her bed is a stuffed rabbit and she blushes when she confides that "a friend gave it to me."

"Things are different out here. You don't have any of the formality that exists in Tel Aviv between officers and the office staff. You have something to say, you say it. This is a very democratic army although, of course, a command is still a command.

"Our morale is very high, partly because we all try to help each other. A girl with a problem can speak to the top officer of the base. You never really feel alone. Last week a girl burst into tears because of a personal problem. It would have done your heart good to see how everyone tried to help her.

"We have a recreation center but when I'm finished with my work, I prefer to be alone. What do I think of? Well, mostly of my dead friends. Silly isn't it?

"When I get out of the army, I want to study. Everyone seems to want to study. You see, if it weren't for the war, most of us would be in school. I don't know what I want to be. I simply want to learn."

You leave Yehudit somewhere deep in Sinai. You pray that time will wash away the memory of blood and that Yehudit will study and learn to laugh, and that her children will face a somewhat different future.

You are barreling down a road in central Sinai when it occurs to you that you may die, but much less heroically than you had imagined. The cause of your troubled reflection is Shimshon, a recruit from the Hatikva quarter of Tel Aviv who has been temporarily assigned to transport you to a new base. Shimshon is angry at the world because his leave has been cancelled and he is tired. What's more, he hasn't had breakfast. Shimshon has already decided that he doesn't like you anymore than he does his corporal who, to quote him, "is a prick."

Shimshon's concept of driving is to lean hard on the gas and to remove both hands from the steering wheel while he chain-smokes and insults fellow drivers. For once in your life, you are too terrified to speak. What a foul way to die, you think.

"Shimshon," you manage to ask, "what were you in civilian life besides a lunatic?"

Shimshon smiles. "You wouldn't believe me if I told you that I was a professional driver?"

You agree with Shimshon: You would not believe him.

"Maybe I was a professor of philosophy," he laughs as the jeep nearly overturns for the twentieth time.

You take a good look at Shimshon. He is a handsome boy of medium build who appears to be about eighteen.

"Give me a cigarette and I'll tell you the truth," he bargains.

You point out that he has a cigarette in his mouth, but Shimshon will not be dissuaded. So you hand him a cigarette which he promptly pockets.

"I was a pimp," he announces.

You smile weakly.

"I'm not kidding," he insists. "I was a pimp and I'll tell you something: without knowing how much you earn, I made three times as much—and remember you're about four times my age—and it was all tax free."

You feel a strong case of heartburn welling up in your chest and you wonder if it's from the speed, the allusion to your age or the disclosure of Shimshon's former career.

"It was really a great racket," continues Shimshon.

"I started when I was fifteen after I quit school. I tried work for a few months, but it made me tired. I figured there was an easier way to get money. Now the one thing I was really good at was screwing. I started playing around when I was twelve and by fifteen I was a champ. So one day it dawned on me that this was the way. I lined up my friend's sister, cut her in for half the action, and I was in business. You know how things develop. Success comes to success. Before long I had three girls stringing for me. I was beginning to get a reputation. I would have had a Mustang by this time if the army hadn't grabbed me. But I'm not sorry about being in Zahal. I'm only sorry about this jerk corporal of mine. I can't wait to meet him when we are both on the outside."

The jeep strikes a rut and you hit the windshield. Shimshon chuckles and points out what the "lousy tank drivers" have done to the road. "Those guys oughta be in jail," he comments.

You ride for another few minutes in stunned silence.

"Give me another cigarette," orders your driver. You refuse.

"Give me another," he winks, "and I'll arrange for a discount."

You thank Shimshon politely but decline his offer. He begins to sulk and suddenly halts the jeep.

"I can't go any further," he says, "I'm too tired. You drive or we'll stay here."

You threaten him, but he yawns and asks for a cigarette. You refuse and take the wheel of the car. Before he falls asleep on the back seat, he smiles innocently and half-whispers, "For you, twice the price!"

The Patrol

The early morning sun curls around your body and feels good. After an almost sleepless night in the bunkers, it is a joy to breath real air again, to be able to move.

Like bats pouring out of ancient caves, small units of men begin to emerge from the bunkers. Many of them are unshaven. They blink against the sunlight. There is almost no talk. If there is anything to be communicated, it is said with the eyes. The men are carrying the tools of their trade—machine pistols, extra canisters of cartridges, hand grenades, communication gear. Laboriously they climb over a wall of armor and enter the armored personnel carrier.

Just behind the driver's compartment of the carrier, one man crouches behind a machine gun. He rubs his palm across a long necklace of bullets. You and the others crouch together on the floor in order to obtain maximum protection from the steel hammered in Moscow and polished in Cairo. While you cock your gun and brush the particles of sand from its barrel, the neighboring citadels are alerted that the patrol is about to commence. There are enough troubles in the world without having Israeli troops firing at you. It would be an ignominious end on such a glorious morning.

An order is dispatched, and curlicues of barbed wire are removed from the entrance of the fort. The men on watch, who have been alerted, are particularly attentive.

The driver, a slim redhead with a smear of oil on his right cheek, enters his compartment and brushes a tiny hill of sand from his seat. He rolls down the movable windshield, cocks his Uzzi and presses the starter. As the motor catches, a junior officer, buckling on his flak jacket, enters the driver's compartment from the right side of the vehicle. He shuts the door hard and latches it. The throbbing of the engine cuts the silence of the fortress, and the officer adjusts the two hand grenades strapped to his web belt. He rises for a second and peers at the crouching shapes in the back. Then, satisfied, he touches the driver on the shoulder and gives the order to move out.

The redhead leans hard on the gas. The sound of the engine in the quiet morning air is an announcement to the enemy of your intentions. The next few seconds are crucial. The vehicle swings hard and your elbow knifes a soldier. Your helmets meet with a dull thud.

"Sorry," you say weakly.

"It's OK," comes the reply.

The vehicle bites into the sand and turns clear of the wire entanglement. A soldier standing on one of the observation posts, his face obscured, waves gallantly at the vehicle. Someone on the carrier shakes his handkerchief in reply.

You turn for a moment and feel a flutter in your chest as the entrance to the fort recedes. Looking into the faces of the young men crouching on the floor, you feel reassured. You would rather be anywhere than where you are, but if you *are* there, then at least with them.

Suddenly the vehicle slows down to an ominous crawl, and the officer and one of the men next to you jump off. They carry their guns cradled as they walk in front of the carrier at a lively pace and prod for land mines with long, thin probes that pierce the dry sand. Meanwhile the machine gunner, peering alertly about, tightens his grip on his weapon. If there is to be an ambush, this is the critical moment.

The carrier is moving at a crawl. The men raise themselves from the floor and take prearranged positions. Every weapon is loaded and ready. In the thin morning sunlight, the entire action takes on the appearance of a slow-motion pantomime. Your stomach growls. A soldier half your age winks at you knowingly.

There is a dull thud behind you and a cornucopia of charred earth is lifted skyward along with a thousand tiny metal splinters. You tighten your grip on the railing of the carrier and feel a film of perspiration between the steel and your hand. Your mouth is dry.

"I guess they haven't had their coffee yet either," someone jokes. "It was a lousy shot. They're usually better than that. It must have fallen seventy-five yards away."

"It's not the coffee," another objects. "It's the food. I hear they're feeding Egyptian gunners on Israeli rations."

"*Gevaldt*," someone else adds, "the United Nations will have us up for genocide."

The conversation is interrupted by the clatter of a machine gun. You turn to the man nearest you and he nods knowingly. "It's just one of our boys giving the

185

Arabs something to think about."

Meanwhile, the two men in front of the carrier continue to prod the earth and the carrier moves ahead over their footsteps. Their composure seems almost inhuman. Except for a vulture hovering over a nearby garbage dump, there are no signs of movement on the landscape.

After the next bend, both soldiers return to the carrier. You notice the perspiration traced down the backs of their shirts. No mines this morning. Even before the two are seated, the carrier convulses into motion and the rear passengers are scrambled together like juggled dice.

"That redheaded bastard is trying to kill us," a soldier mutters.

"Kiss my ass," comes the reply as the carrier furrows deeply into the sand.

The scenery is flat and dull. There are scorched patches of sand where shells have dropped and splintered. There are empty canisters, spent cartridges, scraps of cloth, crushed cigarette boxes, crumpled sheets of newspaper, a canteen ruined by a bullet.

Moments later you raise your eyes and see the Israeli flag flying defiantly over a fortress toward which your patrol is now headed. The flag is shredded and tattered, and the two triangles of the Star of David have been pierced by bullets, but the slice of blue and white cloth floats free. This flag has become the favorite target of every Egyptian gunner and sniper in the area. It has been nailed to the ground by shrapnel more than once, but each time, like the legendary phoenix, it rises into the sky, confirming Israeli's presence on the Canal.

Epilogue

They destroyed the public garden! A single shell tore across the border and the fainting onion sets, the neatly planted mortar shards, the bleached wicker fence were dissolved in a pandemonium of whistling shrapnel and heavy sand. You heard the news over coffee this morning and it filled you with an awful sadness. Amidst the carnage, the little island of mockery and laughter was an oasis of sanity. It will be rebuilt, you tell yourself.

This morning you packed your knapsack to leave Sinai and you thought of how pitifully little man takes to war with him—a few changes of essential clothing, shaving gear, a pen, a canteen you purloined from your oldest daughter, a revolver now gray with grime, a hunting knife. Already, you have returned your flak jacket and helmet. There will be no more patrols—at least for a while.

You are leaving Sinai, and although your skin is burned taut and the sand has coalesced with your flesh and your tongue is bleached white, you are alive and you are returning to a world of hygiene and comfort—a place where there are flowers and smiling children.

You think of your wife and your children and your friends. It seems incredible, standing there in the shadow of war, that in one hour and ten minutes you will be in Tel

Aviv, that you will take a bus north and then you will walk half a mile and you will be home and your combat boots will sink into green, cool grass.

For some reason, you don't want to say goodbye to anyone this morning. There have been too many farewells since you descended from the plane a lifetime ago and sped toward the front. How many have died; how many have been wounded since you arrived? You refuse to think about it.

You slip from the mess hall almost furtively and head toward the mini-airstrip where your plane is expected. It is so early and already it is hot. A cluster of flies dances on your face. You have gotten used to them. You don't even brush them away. Then there is a sudden sound of an engine and moments later Sinai becomes a great orange ball of sweeping sand beneath you.

As the summer of 1970 edged on, however, Soviet missile lines were creeping inexorably closer to a confrontation with Israel. The swollen armories of Alexandria and Port Said were spilling over into the broad swath of desert and bog, comprising the Egyptian defense line. A new type of missile network was being created. The former long, uneven line of SAM-2 missile sites was being replaced by a checkerboard of antiaircraft installations which consisted of SAM-2s and -3s, radar-controlled antiaircraft guns and heavy machine gun nests. New 203 mm guns were added to the arsenal.

In the air, Soviet airmen had replaced Egyptian combat pilots almost everywhere in the country. Both sides were anxious to avoid any direct confrontation but then both sides had adopted inflexible postures. Israel could not permit an Egyptian consolidation in the 20–30 mile zone west of the Canal; the Soviet Union could not permit any further embarrassment to the Cairo regime. There were roughly 12,000 Russians serving directly and indirectly with the Egyptian armed forces.

In northern Egypt, the army of the Nile was training relentlessly for an amphibious crossing. New equipment had arrived in late July and Hassanan Heykal, the mouthpiece of the Cairo Administration, proclaimed the inevitability of a new war, the tempo of which could carry victorious Egyptian forces well beyond the Sinai frontier. The situation was tense in Washington D.C. as well. The new Soviet undertakings had placed war-weary President Nixon in an awkward position. He was desperately anxious to avoid a direct American involvement in a Middle East war which could escalate like a late-summer forest fire.

On midnight of August 7, 1970, a cease-fire fell like a cool shroud along the 100 miles of the Canal. America's peace initiative had been accepted, albeit reluctantly, by the primary contestants. Dust-clogged faces began to emerge from the sand tombs. Flickers of light stabbed the darkness. Shower taps were turned on. Pens began scribbling and mothers began giving thanks in synagogues and mosques.

On the evening of August 8, in direct contravention of the terms of the cease-fire, heavy Soviet trucks began rolling eastward carrying the 35 ft., 4,785 lb. SAM-2. They were being transported by Zil 157 semi-trailer, transporter-erector vehicles especially imported from the Soviet Union. Backing them up were smaller vehicles each carrying a pair of SAM-3 rockets and churning the sand in the general direction of the Canal. What had taken Israel months to accomplish, was being nullified in a single evening. New missile teeth were being fitted into the jaw of the Soviet-Egyptian defense belt. In the next week, the full meaning of the perfidy began to be understood. Not only was Egyptian air space to be protected by Soviet pilots, not only was the entire length of the Canal to be picketed by an awesome accumulation of modern rockets, but the slant range of those missiles was to spill over into Israeli air space and create a nearly intolerable tactical situation. The tactical range of the SAM-2 is about 25 miles; the effective radius of the SAM-3 is approximately 17 miles. The ugly meaning was clear: by violating the cease-fire agreement, Soviet missiles had achieved a measure of control over Israeli air space. Israeli aircraft could be destroyed before they ever approached the border.

Since then the Middle East has been true to form. Fighting with the terrorists erupted on the Lebanese border. The Arab governments of Syria and Iraq continued to call for a "Jihad" against Israel. There has been civil war in Jordan. Nasser's death left many questions. America has provided an additional commitment to supply new equipment, electronic countermeasures and aircraft.

And on the Canal, there has been quiet.

What of the future? It will depend on many factors, political and military. If anything emerges clearly, however, if there is any single message from the Bunkers of Sinai, it is that Israel is prepared to fight, even alone, and that the key to the future complexion of the entire area lies in the desert of Sinai.